Generalities, Truths, & Assorted Fables

Aviation Anecdotes and Adventures

by Daryl Murphy

Jones Publishing, Inc.
N7450 Aanstad Road
P.O. Box 5000
Iola, WI 54945
Phone: 715-445-5000
Fax: 715-445-4053

Generalities, Truths, & Assorted Fables

Aviation Anecdotes and Adventures

by Daryl Murphy

Publisher/Acquisitions Editor:
Gregory Bayer

Editors:
Frank Hamilton, Kim Shields, Gregory Bayer

Art Director/Cover Design:
Kristi L. Skrzypkowski

Cover Art Provided By:
Jeff DeMichiel

Production Team:
Jean Adams, Mikalie Birling, Cindy Boutwell, Cindy McCarville

Published by: **Jones Publishing, Incorporated**
N7450 Aanstad Road
P.O. Box 5000
Iola, WI 54945

Phone: 715-445-5000
Fax: 715-445-4053

This book is available at special quantity discounts for bulk purchases. For prices or other information, contact Greg Bayer at the above address.

10 9 8 7 6 5 4 3 2 1 Printed in the United States
ISBN 1-879825-15-5   **$14.95 U.S. Funds**

About the Author

Daryl Murphy was raised on a Kansas farm. After college, he worked in local television and trade publishing for a number of years before entering aviation in 1965 at Cessna Aircraft Company, where his charge was producing dealer sales shows and promotions.

Murphy left the corporate halls in 1972 and ran a creative services agency in Wichita until 1981, when he became senior writer for an aviation-oriented advertising agency in Oklahoma City. Four years later he emigrated to Dallas to become editor of *General Aviation News*, and in a few years added the title of southwest correspondent for *Aviation International News*, a corporate flight periodical.

His first book, *Flying VFR in Marginal Weather* (published in 1991), was a revised edition of an earlier work by Paul Garrison.

"I assumed the publishers asked me to do the book because of my writing abilities," Murphy explained. "It turns out that I was chosen because they had heard from some of my friends at Cessna that I spent more of my time flying in marginal conditions than any other pilot they knew."

A second book, *Carrera Panamericana: History of the Mexican Road Race*, followed early in 1993 and reflected Murphy's lifelong interest in racing.

He currently lives in Irving, Texas, along with the Dallas Cowboys and his wife of 30 years who is affectionately referred to as "Mrs. Ed" in his "Gadding With GAN" columns that appear in *General Aviation News & Flyer* and this book. ✈

Warning — Disclaimer

Publisher's Note

Jones Publishing, Inc. would like to thank Dave and Mary Lou Sclair, and the rest of the *General Aviation News & Flyer* staff, for their help in producing this book. For more information about General Aviation News & Flyer, write P.O. Box 39099, Tacoma, WA 98439-0099, or call 800-426-8538.

Table of Contents

Preface

Traveling to interesting places all over the country, interviewing famous and fascinating people, and flying their latest creations for free may sound like a little piece of heaven to the "airborn," as ex-*General Aviation News* (GAN) columnist C.D. "Ace" Taylor used to address those who were afflicted with flight. But if you had to spend your days in a sweaty, noisy, cramped aluminum tube shouting questions and trying to hear the answers, writing notes, talking with surly controllers while trying to keep the wheels on the bottom and staying on the glide slope, and then whiling away your nights attempting to think up friendly adjectives to describe some great hog of an airplane, it might lose a little of its romantic appeal.

However, perhaps aviation journalists resemble the airline worker whose sole job was to empty the toilets on every incoming airliner. Because of the location of the drain high off the ground on the underside of the tail section, in the process of opening the valve and fitting a hose to it, some waste would inevitably end up on the man's clothes. In other words, he reeked of it. He complained that people didn't want him anywhere near them; he had to eat lunch alone — way out on the ramp — and he had no friends. But when someone suggested that, if he was so unhappy with his job, he should consider changing careers, he replied incredulously, "What? And give up aviation?"

I was raised near Wichita, Kansas, growing up with a steady flow of Stearmans, B-17s and 29s, T-50s, and Beech 18s roaring over our house. It wasn't until much later that I came to the realization that some people ascribed a certain romance to this armada of fabric and aluminum. I recognized a certain utilitarianism in the objects, but never fully comprehended the truth and beauty of bumping through the skies in a machine made of parts supplied by the lowest bidder and powered by an engine which was likely designed in an era when everyone drove Model As to work.

Early on I discovered that, for me, the people made the whole business/sport/obsession worthwhile. I found that they came in an amazing variety of sizes/shapes/colors/disciplines. They were all unique, and at least 99 percent had an interesting story to tell.

An acquaintance of mine used to be into classic cars — real classics, the kind that are stored in air-conditioned garages and hauled to Pebble Beach in a padded trailer to compete in the *Concours d'elegance*. When I saw him a few years ago at his home in California, he informed me that he was fed up with that hobby; he had sold off most of his collection — including one Ferrari which went for a seven-figure price — and had bought a Stearman in which he was learning to fly. He explained why he was thoroughly enjoying his new avocation:

"It's the people (in aviation). It doesn't matter what their background is, or if they have money; it's their love of the sport. When you're a pilot, it doesn't matter how much money you have. You all have to eat at the same airport lunch counter."

That philosophy struck me as very astute. By and large, we pilots tend not to put other pilots in economic categories. Everyone is judged solely by enthusiasm and/or ability; our business/sport/obsession is blessed with a kind of social blindness.

People are the most interesting part of aviation, and it's been a privilege to meet all these folks seated at the counter. I hope you'll enjoy reading about some of my favorites.

Come to think of it, it's a great job, and I'm proud to have it. And I'm proud to present this book to you.

Daryl Murphy
Irving, Texas
January 1995

Once you can fake sincerity, you've got it made. This photo was shot for a 1990 story as Murphy was about to be strapped into an armed ejection seat to do an hour of dual military-style flight in a Siai-Marchetti S.211 jet trainer. Upon *recovery* (militaryspeak for *landing*), which is a misnomer since he has never recovered from that flight, the photographer wisely declined taking another photo, suggesting that there wasn't sufficient color contrast between Murphy's skin tone and the olive drab flight suit.

Photo by Chris Fairchild

Introduction

This book is a collection of popular "Gadding With GAN" columns. (*GAN* is short for *General Aviation News*.) A lot of you are familiar with the column and its host magazine, but for those of you that are not, following is a brief account of their history.

General Aviation News ("The Green Sheet") was founded in the late 1940s in Los Angeles, CA and got its nickname from the fact that it was printed on green newsprint — a design that was predicated more on the low cost of that shade of paper rather than its distinctive appearance.

After its purchase in the late 1960s by Chuck Wolfe, the popular weekly aviation newspaper was published for more than a decade in Snyder, TX until about 1980 when it was acquired by Taylor Communications and moved to Dallas. Early in 1990 Dave Sclair combined it with his successful *Western Flyer* in Tacoma, WA to create *General Aviation News & Flyer*, which is still alive and well today.

"Gadding With GAN" originated as a weekly column written by Wolfe to chronicle his travels throughout the country calling on advertising prospects and customers, manufacturers, and FBOs. He wrote in a folksy style about people in aviation, and while the columns were often blatant plugs for current advertisers or encouragement to future customers, they nonetheless reflected a great deal about general aviation during those prosperous years.

After The Green Sheet's move to the city of Dallas, the column was retired until the late 1980s, when it was revived as a flight destinations feature written by a variety of contributors. But soon, "Gadding" regained a life of its own, once again featuring the eclectic faces and places of aviation. When the new owner moved the publication to Tacoma, WA, the column was retained.

As the last in an extinguished line of Green Sheet editors, we (the royal personal pronoun normally employed in the column) were asked to continue the feature while traveling on writing projects for *General Aviation News & Flyer* and other magazines. The only restraint was a biweekly deadline. Otherwise, we have been free to indulge virtually any whim that arises, and that has provided a choice opportunity to observe the wide spectrum of aviation people and things around the world, and then share those observations with readers.

Following is a collection of our "Gadding With GAN" columns. The 59 slices of life in this book, which we titled "*Generalities, Truths, & Assorted Fables*," should make easy reading. There's no plot, so you can start anywhere and put it down at any time without losing your place. Put a copy in your flight bag to read while you're streaking through the sky or sitting in an airport waiting for the weather to match your rating.

— Daryl Murphy

1.

Generalities, Truths, & Assorted Fables

In a regular book, this material would be relegated to the back section, under "miscellaneous." This chapter is a collection of pieces that were simply too eclectic to fit anywhere else, but since the stories seem to be the very essence of the "Gadding with GAN" column, we chose to set the stage by putting them first.

Some were actually written "on the road" under primitive conditions (using a manual typewriter or, as in one case, scrawling the story on hotel stationary and then faxing it to the editor); others were written during slow news weeks, or when we were stuck at home after working on a tome which had kept us out-of-pocket right up to deadline. During the latter times, our acquaintances found that their seemingly innocent conversations ended up in print. Eventually that source of material dried up as they learned not to offer opinions, or say anything, that could be quoted, or misquoted.

Cleanliness is Next to Impossible

January

IRVING, Texas — Whilst cleaning off our desk the other day in preparation for a fresh start at the New Year, we came across some things in the left-hand stack (the one which requires attention, but not right away; that's what the right-hand stack is for, while the up-desk center collection doesn't really require any attention, but is comprised of things too valuable to throw away) which have needed our attention.

Starting at the bottom — a process that places material close to its proper historic era without the expense of carbon dating — we found the following items:

• A sign Mrs. Ed (my wife) gave us several years ago. It reads, "A Clean Desk is the Sign of a Dirty Mind." We wondered what had become of that. Frankly, we'd remembered it as reading "Cleanliness is Next to Impossible." It was moved to the up-desk center stack.

• Three different Million Dollar Sweepstakes letters illustrated with Ed

McMahon's picture. Two were from this year, and one from last. Round-filed.

• A free trial subscription letter from *Ag Air Update*, "Ag Aviation's only newspaper," which we immediately filled out and mailed.

• A letter from C.D. "Ace" Taylor, author of the *"Dear Ace — Advice to the Airborn"* series which ran for years in **General Aviation News**. We sent him a Christmas card on January 12.

• A room reservation form for the annual Oshkosh bash, an overdue parking ticket, and a check for two dollars from the IRS. Sent one, paid one, and framed the other.

• Sixty-seven business cards with cryptic notes that seemed important at the time. We have no idea who 65 of these people are or what the messages meant. Filed them under "Miscellaneous."

It's good for the soul, this once-a-year desk cleaning exercise.

For a few moments we stood there admiring the finish on the desk's top, then laid this column on the clean corner.

By the next morning six AOPA news releases, an empty coffee cup and a half-eaten Danish had joined the papers. At noon, a file of photos was perched atop the cup, and three yellow legal pads and a book on hydroponic tomatoes filled the center of the desk. Has anybody seen the Clean Desk/Dirty Mind sign? ✈

New Year's Resolutions

IRVING, Texas — We give a great deal of thought and reflection to the past and future every New Year. Here are some samples of our resolutions over the years. We resolve:

• To continue the intake of an excess of caffeine and cholesterol, in the belief that medical science will eventually prove them beneficial (simultaneous with pronouncing lettuce to be fattening).

• To get an instrument rating without going in the **Guiness Book of Records** for the "highest number of hours/years spent getting an instrument rating."

• To get some dual time in a P-51.

• To make a normal approach and landing without expediting, just to see if it's possible. ✈

Finding Oshkosh for the Geographically Challenged

IRVING, Texas — Well, it's time to start planning for Oshkosh, isn't it? We'll be there in force this year with **GAN & Flyer** and an edition a day.

When Publisher Dave Sclair first told us about it back last winter, we started making plans. After all, Oshkosh is not one of those experiences you can just leave to chance; planning may well be more fun than the actual trip.

When we informed "She Who Must Be Consulted" that she was welcomed — yeah, encouraged — to accompany us, Mrs. Ed was delighted. After years of hearing the accolades of what we consider the best-run, best-attended, most fun convention in the known solar system, she allowed as how she would be honored.

However, before she consented, it was first ascertained that the entire journey would be accomplished with air conditioning and no fewer than four Michelins in contact with the earth at all times. See, she's never shared our enthusiasm for loosing the surly bonds since the time we had a little engine failure due to a lack of fuel management followed by an incident which earned us the unfortunate but eternal nickname, Crash Murphy.

Now, Mrs. Ed is a highly intelligent and infinitely charming person, but one who can be fairly termed as geographically challenged, probably owing to an upbringing in New Orleans, where the only directions are oriented toward the politics of the Lincoln administration. While she can assist nobly in navigation in a mechanical sense, she doesn't have an inborn sense of direction, and what's more, doesn't particularly care. But to her credit, that means she doesn't have to operate under the same restraints as those of us who need to know whence is up on the map.

When you fly, it would seem that efficient, speedy ground-covering is your aim; we once heard Ed Swearingen say to no one in particular, "Why would anyone want to fly unless they could go as fast as possible?" There's something in a pilot's psyche, whether male or female, that demands records be broken, endurance be tested, goals be achieved on every flight (some years back, yrs trly accomplished 750 miles in one day on a motorcycle, the terminus of which was in a proctologist's waiting room).

But when you drive, there are too many distractions. Despite Dad's penchant for striving for some magic number like getting 1,000 miles from home the first day, he inevitably ends up stopping at roadside historic markers and alligator farms and rest stops and pottery outlet stores when he would rather be working toward enshrinement in the Highway Endurance Hall of Fame.

If we were flying to Oshkosh (and it is embarrassing not to), it would be so simple to just point a Skylane to a heading of, oh, about 020 and plan a stop here and maybe there if we have to, and it's only about 1,000 sm—maybe seven hours' flight time. As it is, we'll be plying the interstates and going just a few miles further, but that's not the problem.

"As long as we're going to be on the road anyway" is the subtle way the request starts. "Is it too far out of the way to go to...?" is usually the way it continues. Well, no, Canada isn't really all that far from Wisconsin, as long as we're there anyway; a bit out of the way, but what the hey, if you've never been there, sure, we'll go!

So it looks like before we return to Texas, we will have driven more than 3,000 miles on the roads of eleven states and one foreign country, all because none of them were that far out of the way.

When you come to Oshkosh, be sure to stop by and get acquainted. If you have trouble identifying us, it's easy. She's the cheery, upbeat one that's ready to go to Canada. ✈

Searching the Factory High & Low for the Missing Cardinal Toot Suite

IRVING, Texas — Back 20 or so years ago, when we were but barefoot boys with cheek, we were at the world's largest manufacturer of aircraft, and part of our charge was the movie bidness, making those films that wowed and cajoled the thousand folks who made their living (more correctly, our living) selling the high-wing marvels.

It was, we believe, the second or third year of the Cessna Cardinal, and we had constructed a plot to show the versatility of the bird by presenting the portrayal of a small-time politician who used the airplane for campaigning, accompanied by his secretary and her IBM electric typewriter, and his brother-in-law, who was a pilot. The secretary also led the two-piece band and entertained at each stop, playing a tuba while the pilot tootled a piccolo. We filmed at grass runways all over Kansas, recruiting

The author (circa 1969) peers artfully through the viewfinder of the company Hasselblad on location with the Cardinal.

locals as unpaid extras. While the trio emoted silently, a voice-over pointed out the new and improved features of the aircraft — especially the wide door that allowed the tuba to be repeatedly drug out and stuffed in.

Now during a lull in filming about 50 miles from Wichita, The Boss decided he needed to run back to the office for something, so he borrowed the star of the film, the Cardinal, promising to return post haste. When PH turned to an hour or two, we called to inquire.

"Uh," he stammered over the phone, "I'll be back just as soon as I can find the airplane."

After another hour's wait, the director called a wrap (or whatever it is) for the day, and we all returned to the factory in a severely over-gross 206, and splitting into teams, began to search for the missing airplane. When it became dark, we borrowed flashlights, driving up and down the lines of aircraft at the factory and at the delivery center (in those days, it was not uncommon to have up to a thousand airplanes around the property).

About 10 p.m., feeling that no solution was at hand, we called the Manager of Production at home and asked him to have another airplane ready in the morning—with the same paint and the same numbers as the one that was missing. To our amazement, he agreed. Certain that we were dealing with a stolen airplane, we called the FAA to report the incident.

"Is there anything on the airplane that would help identify it if we should find it?" they asked.

"Well," we answered, "there should be a tuba, a piccolo and an IBM typewriter in the back seat."

"Say again?"

"Tuba, piccolo and typewriter!" We could hear tittering in the tower. "No, seriously," we added as we told our tangled web. They, too, cooperated, although I'm sure not with straight faces.

Having done all we could do, we retired to a local watering hole in town known to be frequented by The Boss, and sure enough, there he was, holding down the bar with his elbows, telling his sad tale to anyone who would listen.

Then about midnight, one of the factory workers appeared, asking for the people who had lost the airplane because he had a message. We pointed The Boss out to him, and the man tapped The Boss on the shoulder and said forlornly, "Sir, they told me to tell you we found the tuba and the piccolo..."

"What? Where?"

"In the back seat of the plane. I guess you musta come in and parked about the time of the shift change, and they put it away way in the back of the paint hangar."

"Whoa," The Boss shouted. "Saved!"

"Just one more thing, Mister," the worker said. "The Manager of Production wants to know if you want the other airplane put on American Express or Bank Americard." ✈

Understanding the Ground After Seeing it From the Air

KILGORE, Texas — We "gadded" to this East Texas town of 11,000 over a recent weekend to visit with Dean and Kathe Miller, old friends from our days in the former Air Capital, where Dean was a faithful Son of Beech and yrs trly a Cessnaite. A fun-filled two days of visiting 300 antique shops in the neighboring towns of Canton, Tyler, Longview, and Gladewater was mercifully interrupted by Dean's award-winning Sunday morning suggestion to eschew church and go flying.

The only reasonable airplane available from Stebbins Aviation at Gregg County Airport was a well-used 150 (what other kind is there?), but after all, our mission didn't require much sophistication. Personally, we had to go to the logbook-before-last to find our latest hours aboard that distinguished model, and when we opened the cute little two-foot by three-foot door and tried to stuff our, uh, mature frames inside, we remembered why.

Flying over the Piney Woods area of Texas was a new experience for us. Statistically about 16 million acres of heavily forested land, its eastern border is Louisiana. As we crossed the town of Uncertain, it was evident that we were near bayou country: nearby Caddo Lake, named after the area's Indian tribe, marks the demarcation of pine trees and the start of cypress. The look and mood of the lake is like a scene from "*The Creature From the Black Lagoon*," and as a matter of fact, that's where the classic movie was filmed.

As is often the case, a flight of this type can reveal a lot about the topography of an area, which adds a great deal to the understanding of its people and its place in the scheme of things. Most evident was the historic town of Jefferson, some 15 miles west of the lake.

During the Civil War, or as it is known locally, "The War of Northern Aggression," Jefferson was a burgeoning city of 30,000 on the navigable Big Cypress Bayou. It had the unique distinction of being a major inland port for the export of cotton to England and Europe, even though it is at least 350 river miles from New Orleans, the closest genuine seaport. Today, its location on the waterway is barely discernible while standing in its historic downtown area, but the vista from an airplane reveals a natural system of rivers, creeks and bayous that made it all possible and practical.

The discovery was as exciting as the first time we saw the Santa Fe Trail from an aircraft over Kansas, stretching for hundreds of miles, following the flow of the land. In both cases the lines on the maps we've studied all our lives are suddenly relegated to merely being visual aids, incomparable to the significance and grandeur of the genuine article.

After such an experience, it was hard to get back to reality, but we had to land mid-sortie at Harrison County Airport in Marshall to investigate a door on the side of our aircraft which had come open during a steep bank and provided an unencumbered view of the woods and water some 2,500 feet below.

When we returned to Gregg County and settled with the FBO for the rental, the young man at the desk greeted us warmly. "Say, you're that fella that writes for that aviation magazine, aren't you?" he asked. As we nodded and smiled semi-modestly, he proceeded to tell us that he read every issue, how much he enjoyed the column, etc., etc., until we were almost embarrassed at the adulation.

"Is it okay if we pay for this by check?" we asked.

"For you? Sure!" he answered with a grin, adding apologetically that company policy required him to get the number off our driver's license.

After we had written the check and provided the proper ID, he stared at them for a long time before looking at us, disappointed.

"I'm sorry," he said quietly, "I thought you were Gordon Baxter!" ✈

Hometowns: Where the Role Models Live

STERLING, Kansas — Growing up in this small town seemed at the time to take a hundred years. Nothing much ever happened, no one famous ever came along, and things seemed to stay pretty much the same year after year. Thirty-five years after leaving, we can now see that those were its best points.

Returning now to take care of family business and do some creative loafing in the Sterling Cafe, it is suddenly clear how — for better or worse — we got here from there.

The revelation came in the form of the retired owner/editor of the local weekly newspaper. We could always spot him on the street because of the ever-present golf cap and long-stride walking pace, uncharacteristic for a five-and-a-half footer who never weighed more than maybe 120 pounds.

You have to remember, a small town editor in days of yore was many things — intellectual guide, local historian, ad salesman, literary critic, resident grammarian, social arbitrator, and even Father Confessor — and to successfully balance all those tasks was truly an awesome feat. But foremost to us was his wonderful talent for editing local tidbits into a column which was not a whole lot unlike this one.

Our conversation soon turned into an interview, although it was not clear who was questioning whom. We were trying to tell The Editor how much influence he had unknowingly provided — an expression which has always been awkward to voice — and he was using his newsman's instinct to guide the conversation onto our subject of interest, aviation and history. He had steered the conversation to talk of TIGHAR and its seeming solution to the Earhart mystery, which had just recently surfaced in the national news.

"Do you remember that airplane that crashed out there in the hills east of town in the Forties?" he asked.

Despite the fact that we couldn't recite our Social Security number, the Great Airplane Crash of 1947 was crystal clear. The "Flying Red Rooster" was famous throughout the listening area of the state's biggest radio station. A solid red Bonanza, it was a traveling billboard, and as it flew between appearances it encountered a thunderstorm and crashed in a remote area around midnight, killing the pilot and his passenger, the station's farm editor.

"I got a call last year from the son of the pilot," The Editor continued. "He was just a baby when it happened, and he wanted to know exactly where his father had died, and if I could direct him to the spot."

Digging out the news reports that he had written at the time of the accident, The Editor narrowed the location to a square-mile area. Not trusting his own memory about the site, he set out to interview people who lived nearby at the time. After several agreements about the approximate location, a team of interested parties was put together, and armed with metal detectors they divided the site into grids and began searching for clues. Success came quickly, and over the next few days dozens of pieces of red-painted aluminum, airframe parts, the carburetor, and a nearly complete seat frame were recovered and identified.

They contacted the son and he visited the site — not out of morbid curiosity, The Editor explained, but from a sense of completing the unspoken and interrupted link with his father. He thanked everyone for their help and then left, noting that he wouldn't need to return.

The Editor had done his part — historian, intellectual guide, Father Confessor, and local contact. No exploitation, no sensationalism, no undue fuss, eschewing platitudes and getting back to normal.

Good values for life. Sometimes it's tough to tell people how grateful you are. But, thanks to them, it's easy to write. ✈

Aviation Olympics

ALBERTVILLE, FRANCE — Watching the Winter Olympics renews an every-fourth-year interest in winter sports for many Americans whose only contact with the white stuff is, at best, under protest. Aside from the re-education of fans about the subtleties of sports like luging, figure skating and hockey, it's also our chance to exercise our patriotism.

It was the latter that came up at the coffee shop the other day. In the best American spirit, how could we insure that we glommed more gold?

"Aviation Olympics," stated one of the group who was a pilot.

"But those ain't athletic events," objected the new car salesman.

"They got events for sailing and shooting," volunteered a retired corrugated box salesman, "and that don't exactly take Mr. Universe to win."

Everyone agreed. As the self-appointed resident expert on aviation, yrs trly agreed that, after pooling the considerable intellectual resources of this cross-section of rabble, we would submit our proposal to the U. S. Olympic Committee — or finish this column, whichever was cheapest.

Consensus was that if aviation was to be included as an event, the following would be representative tests of aviation skills:

The 100-Meter Icy Ramp Race — This event features a cold-soaked J-3 Cub (without starter) parked on a patch of ice. Each contestant would be timed on his (or her) ability to get that sucker started, and then taxied to a finish line 100 yards (or in the Olympic spirit, meters) away.

"Yes, Chris, he got the engine started on the first revolution. I think that's the first time that's happened during these Winter Games. It looks like the German is going to beat the American's time on this one. Wait! He's fallen down while trying to get in the cockpit, and now the airplane is taxiing away without him! If that airplane crosses the finish line without its pilot, it's an automatic disqualification..."

Airport Grand Slalom — Using an approved model with conventional landing gear and at least 300 horsepower, each contestant must negotiate through 50 aircraft parked on an icy ramp, then taxi down a runway bordered by steep snow banks, take off, make one complete circuit of the pattern, land, and then return to the starting point. Whoever does this in the shortest amount of time, wins.

"Well, the Frenchman Giboux is ahead on this one. He's just about to make his landing; his split time is eight seconds faster than the Canadian. Oh, no! He's hit some ice on the runway! Bad luck, but the judges may give him some style points for those toe brake loops!"

The Pentathlon — Flown appropriately in a Decathlon, pilots must complete an 800 nautical mile cross-country within a prescribed time. Additionally, pilots must accomplish the following at the four required fuel stops: **1.** get landing clearance at a major international airport located in a TCA, **2.** comprehend a weather briefing, **3.** purchase and transport auto fuel from a service station or convenience store near the airport, **4.** remove and replace one complete set of spark plugs using only a crescent wrench, and **5.** eat a full meal at an airport cafe during each stop (pilots will be disqualified for using antacids).

It has promise, this Aviation Winter Olympics. While the Nordic countries and the Canadians may have an edge, the American team could be a factor. We're pretty sure the Russians (now that they're from the CIS, what do we call them? Sissies?) can't afford to compete, and that the French would be, well, French. Other countries? We don't see much competition. We haven't yet started to work on the summer games, but we're sure we can create another set of events for that.

Some Other Olympic Thoughts (from 1988): Just think what Sonja Henie could have accomplished if she had used mascara.

The U.S. Olympic bobsled team was the only one to select participants by a tag team match. ✈

2.

Word Games

Some people think that writers should write to the lowest common denominator of their readers — something which could conceivably place their work at about a fourth-grade comprehension level. Before we got legitimate and began our Quest for Truth as an editorial type, we were engaged in the art of composing words for advertising, where the power of simplicity rules.

On the whole, however, we discovered that people who wrote with one and two syllable words and used hackneyed phrases produced pretty pedestrian results, so we decided, while striving to eschew obfuscation, we would also engage our dictionary and spell-checker. So in this chapter, you can read about acronyms, aphorisms, alliteration and other types of etymological endeavors, and if it proves to be too much, take two aspirin and write us in the morning.

Some Autogenous Thoughts About DOT

DALLAS, TX — In the mail January 15 was an announcement from the Office of the Assistant Secretary for Public Affairs, U.S. Department of Transportation (OASPAUSDOT): "Planes must have altitude devices by December 1 at fourteen major airports." At the top of the form letter was the notation, "For release Tuesday, December 1."

Although the story pointed out that "The rule setting the December 1 effective date was announced last January," its arrival 45 days past its release pointed out how the game is played by announcing proposed changes in a manner that will reach the fewest affected parties, and then try to hide it until it can be enacted.

The first word which sprang to mind to describe this cabinet-level agency was *autocratic,* a system which rules with unlimited and undisputed authority. Next came *autonomous,* having the right or power of self-government. Whilst looking up the correct spelling of the former, we found several other words pertinent to the DOT/FAA. They include:

Autodafe—inquisition ceremony along with the pronouncement of judgement followed by execution of sentence, broadly known as the burning of a heretic.

Autogenous — produced independent of external aid.

Autotelic — having a purpose in itself. ✈

Keeping the Art of Aphorism Polished
Requires Constant Attention

DALLAS, Texas — While kicking tires at a suburban airport last weekend, we overheard this colorful conversation between the owner and the prospective buyer of an ancient Cessna 170:

"I don't know, Herb," the first man said, "it's as slick as a watermelon seed, but so slow you'd have to file a flight plan with a calendar."

"Yeah," the seller said as he lovingly ran his hand over the polished aluminum cowl, "but it's as shiny as a deer's eyes in a headlight beam, ain't it? An' as valuable as a herd of pregnant race horses."

Lest you think that these two good ol' boys just fell of the pepper truck and never finished the sixth grade, we should point out that one was a District Court judge and the other an airline pilot. They were using their abilities with aphorisms, an innate talent possesed by most Texans, and one which must be constantly exercised to remain fit.

Following are a few aphorisms we have heard, mixed with some we have modified for use in aviation. Or perhaps we should say we've applied for an STC on them.

Accident Prone — he needs a rubber-lined cockpit.

Accurate as a wind sock.

Appearance, deceiving —just because a chicken has wings don't mean
it can fly.

Arrived — lit and tied down.

Attracted like a doctor to a Bonanza.

Bad Breath — as strong as Jet A

Bald as a radome.

Begin — raise the gear.

Broke — if avgas was a nickel, I couldn't get out of the pattern.

Careful as a welder in a tank farm.

Correct — you got the needle centered.

Crazy — 'bout half a bubble off center.

Departed, left — poked a hole in the sky.

Different as a Cub and a Concorde.

Difficult as passing an FAA ramp check.

Dilemma — lost, but with a great tailwind.

Exciting as a fire at the FAA office.

Failure — he fell off Cloud Nine into a thunderstorm.

Fast — he can fly sunup to sundown in about a half an hour.

Fat — never seen anything that big without Boeing painted on it.

Frightening as a hornet in a cockpit.

Handy as an electric starter.

Hard as flying with water wings.

Hazardous as a blind man standing on ice propping a Cub.

Hot as a vinyl seat in July.

In Trouble — parachuted into a volcano.

Large — a picture of it would weigh five pounds.

No Way Out — flying up a box canyon.

Noisy as a squadron of AT-6s on a Saturday morning.

Out of Place as a Bellanca at a termite convention.

Passenger — window watcher.

Rare as a paid-for airplane.

Release — pull the chocks.

Start — pull the rope.

Surprising as a bolt of lightning from a blue sky. ✈

Acronymic Odyssey Uncovers Ebullient Etymology at NBAA

HOUSTON, Texas — It is possible to exist through the runs of the *NBAA*, *NATA*, *HIA* or *AOPA* conventions without using a noun, we have discovered. The gee-whiz technologies extant seem to require thorough understanding of the acronym, that handy mostly-American penchant to make a new word from the initials or a series of words — *VFR* for Visual Flight Rules, *FBO* for Fixed Base Operator, *GPS* for Global Positioning System, and so on and so forth.

Aviation used to be the champion of the acronym. Bennie Howard's models were always prefixed with *DGA*, which stood for Damned Good Airplane. And the word *radar* is a really useful acronym for Radio Directing and Ranging. You can see why many acronyms are infinitely easier and quicker to remember and use.

When we first entered the inner sanctum of aviation where practitioners spoke this strange shorthand language, it had taken a frustrating spell before we were considered on an intelligence level high enough to participate in many conversations. But we began to use the system upon return from a flight lesson when someone asked how we had done.

"Had my first *PGL* today," we announced proudly. No one acknowledged the reference immediately, but half an hour later one of the more experienced pilots in the group telephoned from the sanctity of his office.

"Uh, just what exactly is that *PGL* you were talking about?" he asked carefully.

"Pretty Good Landing," we informed him triumphantly.

"Oh, yeah, that's what I thought is was," he said, adding quickly, "either that or Pressure Gauge Lag."

At the Enbah convention, or *NBAA* as it is known to some, we were poring over the hundreds of press releases, trying to make sense of the unfamiliar-to-us acronyms which have sprung up since the marriage of the computer and the airplane — both of which have their own specialized acronymic languages and, since the honeymoon, have spawned dozens more terms peculiar to the union.

"Flight Data Centers and Alden Electronics have teamed to provide *RRWDS* information from 102 *NWS* locations," read the product news release. Now in the journalism biz, one is taught to assume that no one knows whence acronyms such as *RRWDS* and *NWS* originate, so in one's first reference to same, one spells out the full set of words followed by its acronym in parentheses. *NWS* was simple — National Weather Service — but while no one would admit to ignorance, no amount of research and/or cryptographic puzzle solving could uncover the solution to *RRWDS*.

The other thing journalists are supposed to do is check facts on someone else's telephone bill, so we called Flight Data Centers (*FDC*) on the toll-free line (*800*). The person with whom we needed to speak was out to lunch, so to speak, so we rung up Alden Electronics (*AE*) and got hold of a person billed as a technical expert (*TE*).

"What in the ever-lovin' blue-eyed world does *RRWDS* stand for?" we asked politely.

"Site radar," the man replied confidently, backing the succinct statement with explanation in some detail of how the system provides information from 102 radar sites on larger airports across the country.

"We understand that," we said as intelligently as we could, "but let us ask it another way: What in the ever-lovin' blue-eyed world does *RRWDS* stand for?" A long silence ensued.

"I don't have the slightest idea," he finally replied quietly.

We speculated that it might be Richmond Regional Weather Data Stuff, or maybe even Ralph's Ribs With Dijon Sauce, or something like that. The man didn't sound amused.

Maybe we should've told him about the *PGL* we had a couple weeks ago. ✦

There are Just Some Things You Can't Do While Reading

NEW YAWK — The Sunday evening flight to Manhattan is filled with the city's natives engaged in the unique ritual of non-stop, cover-to-cover reading of the Sunday *Times*. Virtually every bit of news, features and reviews is digested by its reader and filed away for some future conversation.

Long touted as the authority on everything, that newspaper's reputation is often poo-poohed by most of the hinterland, who think that New Yorkers consider their city the center of the universe, and that politics and business are egocentric and Eastern-centered. The latter may be true. So may be the former. While reading a discarded section of the paper, we discovered things we didn't know about the Superconducting Super Collider, a $14 billion project recently killed in Congress. The Super Collider happens to be located about 40 miles from our Texas home. We also learned that the opening of the Denver airport is behind schedule, and we were just getting into a feature about coal mining in West Virginia when our flight landed at an intermediate stop.

"Hi, there," greeted a boarding passenger. "This seat taken? Whaderya reading? Whatsit about? Any football scores? Don't let me interrupt. I'll just sit here and squirm and make little noises." Obviously, the man was not a New Yorker, or he would have respected the media clenched in our hands. As it was, the sight of any reading material was the universal interpretation of an invitation to commit Timus Interruptus.

In the past, just being able to read was considered an accomplishment. People with this ability were treated with respect and even reverence, and in some societies it was restricted to the elite. Then a few societies, notably ours, got the idea that it was everybody's right, so that we wouldn't have to wait for the elite to tell us what was in the book.

As in many great experiments, it worked very well in the beginning, and even the poorest of citizens read "The Iliad" and "The Odyssey." But with passage of time the prestige and novelty began to wear off, and excessive reading even came to be regarded as a vice ("get your nose out of that book and do something useful"). We described over-readers as "bookish," pale and sickly folk who often walked into trees, had unsatisfactory social lives and seldom married. Gradually, the malady came to be seen as escape from "real" life. It was unconsciously reassociated with the elite class, regarded as an indulgence.

So low has reading fallen, that it is no longer regarded as a legitimate use of leisure time. Real folks would rather be **(a)** watching television; **(b)** taking the kids to the zoo; **(c)** helping the poor; or **(d)** saving the whales.

Of course, television has administered the *coup de grace*. You can watch TV and do almost anything else at the same time. But you cannot read and do anything else, and that includes answering questions about what you're reading.

COLUMBUS, OH, 11:48 p.m. — We were reminded that after a similar trip last spring, we wrote a "Gadding With GAN" column about the efficiency of sometimes taking the airlines rather than flying yourself. We decided this was not one of those times. At this point, our block to block average had been 111.3 mph.

Not really on the route home, we were in Columbus because we had decided to generously donate some frequent flier miles to the cause (they were expiring anyway) and construct an itinerary that would get us as close to our destination as the freebie airline could take us, and then pay for the rest of the trip on some bargain rate.

If our airline schedule would have been a flight plan, the FAA would have likely rejected it as too complex: DAL-TUL-STL-CMH-BNA-LGA. Fortunately for us, on the return trip a helpful ticket agent suggested a more direct route (in airline logic) which required only two aircraft changes and four stops — a resounding improvement over the outbound leg.

On the Nashville-Columbus leg we got to fly on an American Eagle Saab 340B. While some years ago we flew the first production model 340 (with a safety pilot), fooling with aircraft this size is definitely an exception, so our experience on this flight was limited to conversations with pilot Gary Shipman and co-pilot Ted Berrett. Despite the fact that many big-iron pilots look down on the commuters, Gary and Ted (with nine and two-and-a-half years on board, respectively) enjoy their type of flying.

We did, too, but maybe next time we'll look the gift horse in the mouth and rent a 210 for the trip. At least there won't be a guy in the next seat saying something like, "Well, gotta get going now. Let you get back to your reading. Sure looks interesting. Been great talking. We'll have to do this again."

Sure don't see many people reading these days. Wonder why? ✈

Some Things We Say Without Knowing Why

WICHITA, Kansas — In our early youth, it was with some puzzlement that we read poetic phrases like "a soft, gentle rain," and "the breeze wafted through the trees" in literature. In terms of weather in this part of the country, it seems nothing is ever that subtle.

The more common descriptions of weather went like "wind as raw as a whip," "cold as a mother-in-law's kiss," "hot as a two-dollar pistol on a Saturday night," and our personal favorite to describe a downpour, "a real toad-strangler."

It was the latter phrase that set Mrs. Ed to laughing when she heard it muttered by yrs trly. We were waiting in the former Air Capital for some semblance of VFR so we could return our Cessna 182 to its rightful owner in Texas.

"I've never heard that," she said as she wiped the tears from her baby blues.

Even though her youthful years spent in the Deep South could account for that lapse in her education, you'd think after 29 winters as our best co-pilot such a common phrase would have come up once or twice. But she claimed it was new to her.

"Well, what would you call a hard rain?" we asked.

"I'd say it was raining cats and dogs."

"At least a toad-strangler is self-explanatory," we shot back defensively. "How could it be raining domestic pets?"

"You don't know?" she asked. (Don't you just hate it when you consider yourself an authority on something and then some upstart comes along and asks a question that was covered the day you missed class?)

"Cats and dogs are natural enemies," Mrs. Ed explained patiently, as if we were one of her third graders. "You know the expression, 'fighting like cats and dogs?' Well, in a thunder-storm or a heavy rain, it's pretty much the same: the animals represent the conflict of elements."

The luck of the Irish. Within a New York minute we started wondering where some of the words we use came from. With a little research, we found the following lagniappe (pronounced LAN-yap), a custom originated in New Orleans where a merchant gives a trifling gift to his customers with a purchase:

Barnstormer — Actors have long been called "stormers," and in early England when theaters were not available they often performed in barns. However, the name is more appropriate for gypsy pilots who flew low over buildings in small towns in order to stimulate citizens to buy rides.

Boondoggle — This was originally the name of the useless braided leather lanyard worn by a Boy Scout. Later, in the 1930s, it became the term used to describe "make-work" projects of the government.

Blimp — This word originated with the 1914 tests of two non-rigid balloons in England. The "A-limp" model was unsuccessful, but the "B-limp" model was used and thus lent its name to the airship.

O.K. — This term can be traced back to an 1840 election slogan. Martin Van Buren, who was from Kinderhook, NY, was nicknamed "Old Kinderhook" and his supporters adopted O.K. to mean "all right."

Posh — This word can be traced to the practice of rich Britons who, when booking ships to India, would request cabins with perpetual morning sun: Port Outbound, Starboard Homebound — noted as P.O.S.H.

Roger and Wilco — These are WWII aviation radio acknowledgments, probably shorthand for "Received Orders" and "Comply."

Starboard and Port—These originated in sailing. "Starboard" (or steerboard) meant "steering side" because early ships steered from the right side; "Port" was the side which was laid up to the dock for unloading.

WACS, WAAFs, WASPs, WAVES — All these are WWII acronyms for the "Woman's Auxiliary Army Corps," "Women's Auxiliary Air Force," "Women's Air Force Service Pilots," and "Women Accepted for Volunteer Emergency Service."

These little snippets of information can win you a few bets at the local airport cafe the next time it's raining like God pulled the cork, or it's cold enough to make a third-degree Mason drop a degree.

Remember, no other book gives you this lagniappe. ✈

3.

Murphy's Flaws

Thoughts From a Mind That's Like a Steel Sieve

DUMAS, Texas — While visiting with an ag operator in this Panhandle village the other day on the subject of radial aircraft engines — specifically the Pratt & Whitney R-1340 Wasp used on many crop dusters — it occurred to us that the design, which was the company's first, is only a few years older than yrs trly, and that we share a lot of similarities. Built with the same technology, as it were.

For instance, engines of that particular vintage were not equipped with an oil filter as such. They featured only a coarse screen which blocked out the large pieces while sending the rest back to try again

Lately, our memory has begun to resemble an oil screen. It tends to retain only the big bits. While there seems to be enough room to store things like personal identification codes and an occasional phone number, other smaller groups of data such as birthdays, anniversaries, *General Aviation News & Flyer* deadlines and the dates of miscellaneous utility cut-offs slip through the mesh. At least we can remember where to find them. Usually ... if we look.

The R-1340, it is said, is often cantankerous, given to belching smoke and making noise when started early in the morning, clanking along until the oil crawls to the far reaches of the system.

Our personal start-up regimen involves an initial reluctance to consciousness followed by a grudging acceptance of duty. It then requires four cigarettes and four cups of high-test coffee, plus at least one daily newspaper (preferably of conservative bent and with large type faces) before even basic civility can be achieved. Get the idea?

However, once we're going — us and the Wasp — we work diligently and economically. Hopelessly outdated, we nonetheless know our place in the scheme of things and exhibit a fine work ethic — loyal, obedient, trustworthy, etc., albeit at a slower pace than some of the newer models.

It's no bad thing to be remembered for those virtues. ✈

One Curmudgeon's Cynical View on Corporate Cannibalism

June 1993

WICHITA, Kansas — The Air Capital used to be a product of its own time and place, full of innovators and self-made companies.

Walter Beech, Clyde Cessna, Lloyd Stearman, Bill Lear, Al Mooney and dozens of other familiar aviation legends put the town on the map. So did the Colemans and the Carneys, they of lanterns and pizza (as in Hut) fame.

Granted, a lot of the aviation pioneers were better engineers and pilots than businessmen, but in any case, the point became moot when the age of their kind of entrepreneurship ended in Wichita along with the seventies. That's about the time previously unthinkable acquisitions began to be made—Raytheon took over Beech, General Dynamics got Cessna, and Learjet ended up owned by something called Integrated Acquisitions. The aviation experts who had built the industry were replaced by financial experts who effectively analyzed it into submission.

The latest case of corporate cannibalism is unfolding in the Air Capital as Beech's parent, Raytheon, is closing a reported $400 million deal for the corporate jets unit of British Aerospace.

While Beech was founded, and prospered early on, with innovative product design, the design times seem to dictate that the most economical avenue to tomorrow's marketing success is "badge engineering." That is, putting a Beech hood ornament on someone else's airplane, which is how the MU-400 came to be called a Beechjet.

Of course, if there is one airplane in the world which has had more type names than the BAE 125 series, we would like to know what it is. Premiered in 1965 as the DH (De Havilland) 125A, it also would be known over the next 28 years as the Hawker-Siddeley, British Hawker and British Aerospace 125, or in the vernacular, simply the "Hawker." It was even marketed briefly in the United States by none other than Beech, which had earlier tried unsuccessfully to market the MS-760 Paris Jet.

Acquisition 101

Despite what the current acquisition/consolidation mindset is, it is probably without regard to historical precedent. It seems as if each generation tries to reinvent the wheel and claim it as its own, only to find out the original patent is still good.

One of the originators of the acquisition genre had to be Avco. When T.H. Embry and John Paul Riddle won a mail route in 1929, Sherman Fairchild offered the flying service a loan to ensure that Embry-Riddle would keep selling and using his aircraft.

Fairchild, not a particularly astute businessman, asked his board of directors to appropriate $1 million. The board went to Wall Street and found that they could just as easily get 35 times that much money in those free-and-easy days before Black Monday, so they did, forming a new company called the Aviation Corporation. Then they began to look for other aviation plums that had fallen off the tree.

The first fruit picked up by the board was the Fairchild Airplane Manufacturing Company. Over the next few years, Avco acquisitions totaled somewhere from eight to 85 companies (no one was ever sure of the number), among which were five airlines (including American). Three of the airlines were holding companies themselves, controlling 11 carriers.

Avco also picked up Lycoming Motors, Stinson Aircraft, Smith Propeller and at least two airports: Roosevelt and Curtiss fields on Long Island. By 1935, investigators trying to sort out the morass of subsidiaries wrote in a 24-page report:

"On some old organizational charts, the names of some companies are found but we never have been able to find the companies, and in at least one case we have found a company which apparently belongs to (Avco) but about which we have been able to find nothing."

Let's hope that the merger-crazed nineties do not create this same scenario. Clarence Darrow once said, "History repeats itself, and that's one of the things that's wrong with history."

Our advice, though, is this: Those who do not believe history are doomed to repeat it. ✈

A Penchant for Being in All the Wrong Places at All the Right Times

IRVING, Texas — Yrs trly has a penchant for being at the wrong place at the right time — actually, in the right place at the right time, but without realizing it. Over the years, we have managed to meet enough famous people to satisfy even the most compulsive name-dropper.

Take last week. We ran into Herschel Walker at the Fed Ex office. Well, maybe "ran into" is not entirely correct, or we wouldn't be able to write this column today. The man is solid. The 1982 Heisman Trophy winner from Georgia came to Dallas to play for the Cowboys. A few years ago he changed into a Viking from the North Country, but he elected to keep his home in Irving, where he has been a civic asset to the community.

The week before we were in Chicago trying to drive our rental car out of Meigs Field when police stopped us. My daughter — who obviously inherited the wrong-place/right-time syndrome — asked a Secret Service-looking man in mirrored sunglasses and comfortable shoes what the occasion was.

"VIP dedicating a statue," was the curt reply.

"Oh? Who is it?"

"I'm not at liberty to say, Ma'm!" he said in his best Joe Friday voice as the police escort wailed and screeched into the drive. It was obvious from the vice-presidential seal on the doors who was in town, and Dan Quayle and family quickly emerged. After a brief ceremony, the entourage left. (We heard one semi-impressed tourist comment, "Wow! That was exciting...Who was it?")

Several years ago, Frank Robinson (of the helicopter company with the same name) introduced us to one of his long-time valued European customers. We didn't quite catch the name, but visited at some length with the distinguished elderly gentleman with the German accent. In the next day's issue of *HAI Convention News*, we learned that it was Adolph Galland, the World War II ace and Luftwaffe commander.

When we visited Cessna's Reims, France facility back in the '60s, it was headed by Pierre Closterman, famous French underground hero and leading WWII ace — the latter a fact we didn't know until some months later when a war plane buff we knew nearly fainted when we mentioned we had met the man.

We recently spoke with Kevin Costner ("Excuse me! Can I get through here?"), Paul Newman ("Oh, I'm sorry! Did I hurt your foot?"), Van Cliburn ("Do you know Melancholy Baby?") and the Archbishop of Canterbury ("No, J.R. Ewing isn't actually a member of this parish!").

Thinking back, we may have inherited this proclivity from my father. Years ago — sometime in the late '30s or early '40s — he was in Wichita to attend some sort of meeting and was in the lobby of the Lassen Hotel when he noticed an inebriated man preparing to relieve himself in an ashtray placed by the elevator doors. Dad quickly went to the befuddled man's aid and steered him to the men's room. Thanking my father profusely for the action to retain his dignity, the man produced his business card and scribbled his signature on the back.

"If you ever need anything — anything at all — be sure and give me a call," he said as Dad helped him to a waiting car.

After the man left, Dad looked at the card. The well-dressed drunk was a world-famous aviation personality — a legend even then — but my father never capitalized on the occasion. He kept the card and the story to himself until the man had been dead for at least 30 years.

After all, Dad said, the poor man was simply in the wrong place — but at the right time. ✈

I'm Sorry. Someone Else Was Using the Pencil

IRVING, Texas — "I would have written this sooner, but I got a Christmas tree ornament stuck in my pancreas and it kept winking on and off, and I was too distracted," alibied author E.B. White to a friend. And Dorothy Parker, offering an excuse to her editor after he confronted her for spending an afternoon at a bar rather than in her office writing, said "Someone else was using the pencil."

These two are gems from a book a well-meaning friend gave us last week. She had won it as a door prize at a laundromat opening or some other important social event. Titled *Excuses, Excuses: A Compendium of Rationalizations, Alibis, Denials, Extenuating Circumstances and Outright Lies* (Penguin Group, NY, 1992), she thought it would be useful, explaining that we could undoubtedly put it to a noble use.

Already we have adapted several of the more creative alibis with some mixed success:

• *I know I was scheduled for my BFR Tuesday, but Saturn's in Scorpio this month; I can't cope.*

• *I never got your message. The cat peed on the answering machine a couple of weeks ago and it hasn't been working right ever since.*

We've been waiting for an opportunity to use the following line attributed to Assistant Secretary of State Elliott Abrams when asked about his involvement in the 1987 Iran-Contra scandal: *I never said I had no idea about most of the things you said I said I had no idea about.*

We don't mean to make such weak excuses, do we? But faced with an unexpected question, most of us aren't willing to reveal the truth about why we were late, absent, unobservant, forgetful, or just plain stupid.

Take President Nixon's 1973 explanation for why one of the key Watergate tapes had a mysterious 18-minute erasure: *Oh, that was just an accident that happened.* Or Bill Clinton on his admitted use of marijuana in college: *I didn't like it and I didn't inhale it.*

The NTSB accident reports are brim full of great alibis, many of which must have sounded good when first uttered:

• *All three lights were green; something had to have gone wrong with the landing gear.*

• *The wind shifted 180 degrees while I was on final.*

• *The fuel must have leaked out after I did my pre-flight check.*

The "Little White Lie," conceived between the time you climbed out of the airplane and before (check one) ❑ *your wife/husband*; ❑ *your instructor*; or ❑ *the FAA* arrived, may seem increasingly credible as you practice and refine it in your own mind. But, once blurted out for the world to hear, it suddenly sounds facile, improbable, and idiotic.

But don't despair. Most of the people, having heard your own excuse, have already filed it in their minds for future use.

There are, according to **Excuses, Excuses...** by author Leigh W. Rutledge (who says he lives in Pueblo, Colorado and spends his days finding excuses not to do his chores), several maxims to alibiing:

A. The feebleness of an excuse should never be a deterrent to its use. (e.g., *I couldn't find the frequency for the tower.*)

B. Always put the blame on something that cannot defend itself: children, pets, inanimate objects and foreign relatives are always good. (e.g., *The sun was in my eyes!*)

C. Certain ailments work better as excuses than others (no doctor in the world can prove that you *don't* have a headache).

And finally, try to remember that Nature allotted each of us only two grandmothers to attend funerals for. ✈

Sometimes it's Easier to Take a Boeing 757 Than the Ol' Cessna 172

NEW YORK—The last two weeks have been fraught with a lot of travel, good intentions and unfulfilled missions. Because of some miscellaneous commitments to nonprofit causes (the bona fide, tax-exempt type, not those unsuccessful little ventures we invest in from time to time), we added nearly 6,000 miles to our Frequent Flyer account while attending a succession of meetings. And we did it entirely in the aluminum tubes of the nation's airlines—for about 25 cents a mile.

Why, you ask, did we eschew general aviation, the very genre from which we draw our sustenance, our life's blood? If you have to ask, you may have entirely too much time on your hands (and as a friend once pointed out, "Owning an airplane may be God's way of telling you that you have too much money").

While a noble thought, traveling 6,000 miles in a Cessna 172 or something equivalent in which we are current and qualified would consume a little more than six eight-hour days of flight time and multi-thousands of dollars.

There are simply times when you should ask dad for the keys to the 757.

The closest we got to visiting general aviation was in Tampa, Florida. We glanced at our ticket and saw that the flight did not leave for the next destination until 7:30. With several hours apparent leeway, we had planned to visit the Executive Beechcraft operation, but closer examination of our ticket revealed that it was Flight 730 leaving at 4:10, not the reverse.

The next weekend found us in Charlotte, North Carolina with all the good intentions of stopping by Thurston Aviation to check on the state of their business, but a well-meaning acquaintance booked lunch on Sunday in the restaurant atop the stands at the Charlotte Motor Speedway, and we spent all afternoon transfixed by the sight and considerable sound of NASCAR wannabes circulating the driving school's 1.5 mile banked track at 140 mph.

The final justification of the 757-versus-172 question was succinctly answered as we returned home amidst world-class thunderstorms and tornadoes, flying what must have been a 500-mile arc from Shreveport to Dallas (a straight-line distance of 150 miles) in zero visibility at 35,000 feet! We have always made it a rule to do neither of those things in a 172.

However, the next day we did get to visit Alliance, the Perot Group's industrial airport near Fort Worth. The occasion was the arrival of a contingent of perhaps 50 government and industry officials from Russia aboard a 300-passenger Ilyushin 96 on its first transatlantic crossing, a 12.5-hour flight from Moscow. The group was in town to promote a cargo operation to the airport, and while it was treated to good, old-fashioned boots-and-hat Cowtown hospitality for several days, we can assure you that no one mistook any of the visitors for guys named Slim and CJ. ✈

Genius May Be in the Details, but the Truth is in the Timing
November 1993

IRVING, Texas—"You can't have opinions about truth," Tommy Smothers once told his brother, who had questioned the basis of a fantastic tale.

Maybe not, but in the news media biz, the truth is sometimes in the timing.

With the holidays inevitably coming, editors and columnists begin to reason that with all the parties and disrupted deadlines, perhaps a retrospective look at highlights of the year would be in order. And as usual, on our way to find one thing, we discovered another.

Leafing through the files of columns past, we found an alarming number of

*We predicted the first flight of the **Swearingen SJ-30** in the fall, then missed the occasion in February.*

reports under our byline with out-and-out errors, or stories that concerned products and programs which ultimately did not come to pass as predicted.

One of our earliest errors in judgment was made on the 1964 introduction of the Learjet, when we espoused that "Nobody in his right mind would spend $500,000 on a business jet." (Fortunately, the pronouncement was vocal rather than in print, so it can be denied.) Then in the '70s, we picked five of our all time favorite aircraft models. By 1980 only one was still in production.

We committed another error in judgement about four years ago when we reported Tom Casey's round-the-world flight from Seattle in a Cessna 206 floatplane. Seemingly a perfect public relations vehicle for general aviation, we jumped into the story with both waders. As you may remember, the plan was to fly west across Russia and Europe and thence the Northern Route to the U.S. and back across to Seattle, becoming the first general aviation airplane to fly around the world landing solely on water.

When Casey was refused entrance to Russia, he decided to just turn right and hope permission was granted by the time he got around the other side of the globe, which was planned for some 30 days later. Well sir, while navigating the Middle East, he injured himself and decided to spend a few days in the hospital recuperating. The fact that he chose Jeddah, Saudi Arabia on the eve of the Gulf War was unfortunate, but by now almost predictable. Weeks later, he set off across Southern Asia, still hoping to get into Russia so he could make a short hop to Alaska. Not to be, so he flew to the ragged edge of the Cessna's range from Japan to the Aleutians. The next day he blew his engine. *In toto*, not a public relations coup for general aviation.

Then we introduced the fictitious L.G. Poteet, an outrageous Texan who supplied us with editorial opinion from time to time. In a piece explaining why higher fuel prices didn't make any profit for the FBO, we wrote that we ran into him while he was fueling his Lear at Staci's Jet Center, which is an Exxon dealer. Unfortunately, the idea for the column came from Ed Blair at Triton — an Exxon competitor.

We repeatedly and incorrectly predicted the first flight of the Swearingen SJ-30 to be "any day now" starting in September 1990 and then missed the actual February 1991 event.

We incorrectly accused TV's "Northern Exposure" of using an Aeronca and identifying it as a Cessna. (We forgot that the early 140 had two double-wing struts.)

Found out from a Delta 757 driver that the accepted and preferred crosswind method is to crab, not cross-control — despite what the *General Aviation News & Flyer* "Flight Instructor" columnist said, and not to mention what we wrote in our book, "*Flying VFR in Marginal Weather.*"

Kept promoting the Ishida tilt-wing aircraft as the wave of the future. "It will be another three years," we gushed, "but it looks like you can bet on it happening. Such is the confidence that well-organized, patient builders provide." In fall of 1993, the program collapsed.

We have become cynical by nature and experience in order to protect ourselves. We don't mean to be spoilsports, but whatever the proposed project is, chances are that we've been through it before: once, twice, a hundred times. However, sometimes there are plans that come across our desk looking so good and positive that we publicize them for the good of the industry.

We may know from experience that it only has an outside chance of making it in the market, but nonetheless we report it as upbeat as possible, hoping that some angel will be attracted to come along and dump millions into the project so that it will come to pass. And also so we can say we predicted it would succeed.

In the business, it's called the Bede Syndrome. ✈

Tilt-Wing: Just the Thing to Become a Complete Aviator

FORT WORTH, Texas — An interesting place to be these days, this cowtown which is often compared to Wichita. Besides being linked by the Chisholm Trail, the two similar-size cities share a lot of common cultural and business interests — the latter including aircraft. The Fort Worth area has LTV, General Dynamics, Bell Helicopter, Textron; Wichita has Beech, Boeing and Cessna Aircraft (Textron), among others.

While the "Peerless Princess of the Plains" boasts an uncommon number of fixed-wing products and pilots, down in Fort Worth — "Where the West Begins" — a large number of products and people tend to orient their flying vertically. That is, until recently. At least some of the future flight in this neck of the woods is likely to be in mixed media: Bell is fine-tuning flight and funding of its touted V-22 tilt-rotor, while across town at Alliance Airport, Ishida is convinced that tilting the wings is the answer.

It's a classic confrontation. Besides the differing design and operation philosophies, the two companies are talking to two different markets: Bell and partner Boeing are counting on government dollars to absorb the development shock via military sales (it seemed like a good idea when the program started), while Ishida will depend upon civil sales to recoup its costs.

"That's the tack that's been taken," said Ishida's Vice President of Engineering John Stowe about the V-22 program, "and in that large an aircraft, it almost has to be. If you developed it civil, you could never market it for enough money to hope to ever break even. The smaller an aircraft is, the easier it is to do."

The V-22 is large—a 47,500 lb. vertical takeoff weight, rising to 60,500 lbs. for short rolling takeoffs. The Ishida TW-68 will operate vertically at 14,000 lbs., and 16,500 lbs. STOL.

Corporate philosophies aside, we asked Dorman Cannon, director of Ishida's flight operations, just who he expected would be flying the tilt-wing when it's certified. (Helicopter pilots are a dedicated lot. According to the FAA, there are more than 8,800 helicopter-only pilots currently licensed, with roughly only another 10 percent who are additionally rated fixed-wing.)

"I think that when a customer comes to us," Cannon said, "our first question (to the pilot) is 'are you rated in airplane and helicopter?' If he's not, he's going to have to get that other rating." Speaking to those with rotor-only ratings, Dorman suggested, "the tilt-wing or the tilt-rotor is not the place to try and learn airplane-associated problems like stalls. It suffers the same maladies that an airplane does — and the same ones as a helicopter."

One can quickly see the problems associated with the new genre. For example, fixed-wing aircraft have fixed incidence of wing, while a tilt-wing has whatever incidence you want it to have. Whereas airplane drivers gauge takeoffs and approaches by relation of the nose to the horizon (real or artificial), by swinging a wing up, the airplane will slow and descend while the fuselage remains level — or even nose-low.

"The notion about moving your thrust vector to accelerate and gain speed — or conversely change your thrust vector aft so as to decelerate and stop — is easily adaptable," Cannon explained. He then added matter-of-factly, "While I've only flown the AV-8 *Harrier* on one flight, I found it was easy to adapt to."

The man obviously knows whereof he speaks. His 25 years at Bell included involvement in the tilt-rotor program, and he has flown both the XV-15 and V-22 prototypes.

"I've been flying since 1953, but I still consider myself a restricted aviator," he said. "I think a complete aviator would want to fly a tilt-wing or a tilt-rotor because it's such a thrill." ✈

The Art of Collecting: Knowing What to Discard

DALLAS, Texas — Some people are natural accumulators, like yrs trly. Others are put on earth to keep order, duties of which include throwing out seemingly useless articles. For better or worse, Casa Murphy houses one of each character type.

We attribute our personal packrattedness to a rural background. Everything was saved because **(a)** you never knew when it would be needed, and **(b)** in the country, nothing ever went away—the wages of having no weekly trash service.

Primarily because the savers outnumber the tossers, America has become a nation of collectors. And, generally, collecting evolves into specialties, whether that is Menasco-engined aircraft or cocktail napkins from Nevada bars. But given

Pilot licenses issued to Glenn Curtiss by the Aero Club of America *(left) and* L'Aero Club de France, *dated October 7, 1909.*

the fiscal limitations of most of us, our hoarding leans toward the more ordinary articles, where volume can displace discernment.

It was that very problem of bulk which lead, indirectly, to the acquisition of some of the most valuable artifacts now housed in the History of Aviation Collection (HAC) at the University of Texas in Dallas.

According to George Haddaway, former publisher of **Flight** magazine and founder of the collection, Jerome Fanciulli wanted to donate what he considered significant items to the National Air and Space Museum. He had saved these items during his tenure as a sales rep at Curtiss Airplane Co. Faced with limited space and hundreds of similar offers every year, the museum said, "thanks, but no thanks." The collection found its way to Dallas and the HAC, and while it contained a great number of invaluable artifacts, there were two which were, for want of a better term, priceless. These were Glenn Curtiss' American and French pilot's licenses. Although there are no numeric notations, they were the world's first.

George took the two leather-bound cases from their locked display. Us hold them? No. It is more appropriate, we mused, to photograph these icons in the hands of the ordained.

Other collections fill out the library's considerable shelves, but perhaps none more rare than the fruits of Haddaway's 60 years of collecting: first editions which include books dealing with the Montgolfiers' balloon flights (1783), Sir George Cayley's gliders (1809), and Otto Lilienthal's **Der Vogelflug** studies (1889) which taught the Wright Brothers to approach flight in a methodical and scientific manner.

"If you're going to name the greatest flights in this century, of course you'd have to start with the Wrights' because they made the first powered, sustained flight," Haddaway reckoned. "But aviation didn't amount to a hill of beans until 1908, 1909, 1910, when Glenn Curtiss came along and picked up the ball."

It's probably no coincidence that George Haddaway became such a promoter of aviation, and friends with many of its pioneers. It was almost preordained; he was born on July 25, 1909, the day Louis Bleriot became the first to fly an airplane across the English Channel.

Haddaway's baptism of flight was at the age of 11 with a barnstormer who was a neighbor in Fort Worth. George started taking lessons when he attended the University of Texas. "That was the end of (my) ordinary civilized life," he added.

Despite the heroic feats in early aviation, he contends that most of the pilots were motivated by prize monies.

"When Bleriot landed in France, the constabulary came to arrest him to see if he was carrying any contraband; they weren't interested in the fact that he'd broken records. And when the Frenchmen Blanchard crossed the Channel in a balloon in 1785, he had to beat off a hitchhiker with an umbrella — the first air piracy. You see why I'm interested in air history?" Haddaway asked rhetorically. "It's just full of human nature. And genius."

The newest addition to the History of Aviation Collection consists of papers and memorabilia from an old friend, the late Jimmy Doolittle. While the HAC is already recognized as one of the premier research libraries in the world, plans call for expansion with the Doolittle Military Aviation Library collection.

We doubt that license #1761300 will ever achieve museum status, but we'll certainly keep it for future generations to view, along with a 1969 Cessna 172 brochure, a complete collection of NBAA name tags dating from 1982, and a canceled check endorsed by Jim Bede. You never know. ✈

4.

Doings in the Aviation Capitals

It used to be that Wichita, the "Peerless Princess of the Plains" (or "Doo-Dah" as a local columnist dubbed it), was the Air Capital. During those halcyon days, 40 or 50 shiny new airplanes rolled out the doors of Beech, Cessna, and Learjet every working day of the week. Wichita was also home to Boeing and its collection of subcontractors, and had once housed Laird, Mooney, Stearman, and a hundred others. There was no doubt about it — Wichita was aviation's Mecca. Then, for manifold reasons, that economy folded. Nowadays, the AirCap is wherever the action is.

The World Didn't Stop When Cessna Quit Buying Piston Engines

WACO, Texas — RAM Aircraft Corporation may not have invented the liquid-cooled aircraft engine, but they are certainly today's champion of the beast. Their mating of Continental's TSIOL-550 "Voyager" with Cessna's 414 has renewed interest in both liquid cooling and the no-longer-produced twin.

Teledyne Continental Motors (TCM), which had been toying with the genre for some time, built a 110 horsepower, four-cylinder engine which Burt Rutan used rather successfully to power *Voyager* on its epic nine-day, around-the-world flight. The design originated around 1979 in a secret military drone program that required extremely high and efficient operation. To that end, a pair of T-300 170 hp turbocharged Voyagers powered an unmanned Boeing research aircraft that set an altitude record for piston engines at 69,980 feet.

We "gadded" down to Waco to visit with Jack Riley, Jr., founder and president of RAM Aircraft. We had read TCM's hyperbole about the Voyager series, but wanted to get the opinion of the man who knows most about them in actual service (RAM's 414AW is the TSIOL-550's only certified installation).

"Liquid cooling solves several problems," explained Riley. He said that air cooling begins to be a problem above 20,000 feet. The air is thinner, so an increased volume is required to dissipate the heat. Airplanes such as the 414A that are designed with tightly fitted cowlings are particularly susceptible, and liquid cooling offers an answer to the dilemma. Further, because the engine's internal temperatures can be controlled more precisely with liquid cooling, closer piston-to-cylinder bore tolerances are possible. "This lets you have higher horsepower in the same size package. Also by liquid cooling you effectively eliminate thermal shock on power reductions and rapid descents."

The 414AW (the "W" is for winglets) uses the 350 horsepower TSIOL-550, which is a dead ringer for the TSIO-550 except the air-cooled cylinders have been replaced with water-cooled cylinders and associated plumbing. Besides gaining 40 horses per side on the twin, the operator has also gained several hundred hours to a 2,000 hour TBO — pretty good reliability for that much horsepower.

The proof is in the flying: higher gross and payload weights, and better climb performance and operating speeds—224 knots at 17,500 feet at 75 percent power (versus the 414A's 204 knots), and 244 knots at 30,000 feet. About the only operational difference is the elimination of cowl flaps and the addition of water temperature to the instrument scan.

"These planes were such a good product to begin with that they're not being junked or abandoned," said RAM sales manager David Seesing. "They (aircraft owners) are now realizing the value of 340s, 414s and 421s—these people know what they have."

RAM's bread and butter business is basically restoration, said Marketing Services Director Chuck Morrow. "People have made a decision that they like their airplane and they want to keep it." RAM engines come in several stages of power, and the company concentrates solely on TSIO-520-powered models — plus the TSIOL-550 installation. Engines are available to a network of dealers, and the Waco operation will handle 100-110 airplanes per year.

"You know, the world didn't stop just because Cessna quit building (these) airplanes," Morrow wryly observed. ✈

Aircraft Sales are Alive and Well in Southeastern Colorado

LAS ANIMAS, Colorado—Of all the places to find a booming aircraft sales center, this smallish town some 85 miles east of Pueblo would seem the most unlikely. Situated in the Arkansas River Valley, the local landscape is a band of green fields set in the middle of brown nothingness. Irrigation canals supply water to crops on a narrow band of farms bordering the river.

As in most dry climates, the farms, ranches, and even cities can tend to look a little junky and cluttered. It's not because the natives are slobs; the main reason is that a lack of vegetation leaves little to hide things behind. It's hard to discard cast iron things out on the prairie — they just don't go away.

The open-sided hangars at the Las Animas Airport didn't mask much, either. A Citabria here, a Cessna 172 there, an AT-6 with its wings off — fairly typical of a small airport. Wait! That was no AT-6! It had tricycle gear!

We wheeled into the office attached to the largest hangar, where Joy Thayer of Variety Aircraft, Inc. greeted us.

"Is that a Yak?" we queried.

"Yes, it's a Yak 18A," she answered. "The other one is in the hangar — would you like to see it?"

The Other One was the finished version, a faithful restoration in its Chinese colors and markings, with a 285 horsepower PZL nine cylinder radial — complete and ready for sale at $55,000.

Variety Aircraft, Inc. had done the restoration, but that's not their main bag, Ms. Thayer said. Selling airplanes is, and as a matter of fact, her husband Jim was in Ulysses, Kansas at that very moment doing that very thing. And when he came back they were leaving for a trip to the West Coast for about a week.

Seven days later, we talked with Jim on the telephone.

"Hi, Jim, got a few minutes?"

"Gosh, I sure don't. We just got back. We picked up an airplane in L.A. and two in Sacramento and now we're headed for Phoenix. Let me give you to Bill Marlman. He can tell you anything you want to know. "

We had met Marlman when we were in Las Animas, and while he carries the title of vice president, he insisted he was retired. Bill built the airport in 1942 and has operated there ever since. He taught several generations of Coloradans to fly, including Bonanza speed merchant Mike Smith, who grew up in Los Animas.

"Yeah, Jim just got back last night with a Cessna 337, a Baron and a Bonanza," he said. "He'll move as many as 80 airplanes a year — mostly light twins and singles, but he's had some Citations and a couple of DC-7s. "

Marlman went on to explain that most of their selling is done in the central and western parts of the country, but some of the buying is done quite aways from home.

"Last year he bought four 400 (Piper) Braves in Sweden. He got a Bonanza in Japan and had it flown home, and he bought eight 414s in Hawaii and brought them back." Pretty heavy stuff for a small town operation.

But why Las Animas, Colorado? From a personal standpoint, all of its 2,800 people likely know Thayer and Marlman; the airport is between two and five minutes from anywhere in town; and there's no TCA to worry about.

From a business standpoint, aircraft sales is not as location sensitive as in past years. The telephone and the Fax machine have replaced a lot of running back and forth.

But Marlman may have best summarized the reason aircraft sales are alive and well in Southeastern Colorado: "It's a good, cheap place to operate from. "   ✈

There's More Than One Way to Make Money in General Aviation

WICHITA, Kansas — In town for the rollout of the new Learjet Model 60 a month or so ago, several of us aviation writer types were comparing notes so that we didn't duplicate our prose in competing publications. We got to talking about the good ol' days in Doo-Dah, when an endless variety of models were pouring out the doors and a press junket to Beech or Cessna to fly the new and/or improved goods was a twice-monthly thing. Our nostalgic discourse probably had something to do with the fact that during this economically disadvantaged age, we were having to pay our own bar bill.

"Well, it could have been worse," suggested Joe, a member of the distinguished group. "They could've actually put all the airplanes on the market that they built."

We nodded sagely, remembering the Beech whatsitsname and that Cessna thing with the shrouded prop.

"Really?" chirped a younger, more idealistic writer who hadn't joined our chorus of nodding . "Like what?"

"Well, I remember Cessna flying around in a Chevrolet Corvair-powered 150," he began, "trying to make up their minds about using it — and that was six months after GM dropped it. And then there was the Olds V-8-powered 175."

We settled back as Joe sucked an olive off its toothpick and looked into his distant memory and chewed.

"Then there was Beech's model 34 back in '47," he continued. "High-wing. Looked like a pregnant porpoise. V-tail, with four 400-horsepower GSO-580s driving two props. Could carry 20 passengers to maybe 300 mph. Problem was, they found out it was cheaper for a customer to buy a surplus DC-3, so when the prototype bellied in, they just junked it.

"Then in '53, Cessna got the idea that they could do it better than Beech, so they built the 620 — four 350-horsepower GO-526s, a six-foot-high cabin, onboard APU and a 400-gallon fuel capacity."

"Wow!" the young man exclaimed. "What happened to it?"

"They found out the same thing about the market that Beech already knew, so they junked it. Then in the '60s, they built the 160, which used beading on the fuselage and wings for strength, and they made it cheap to build. They saved it a couple of years, then — junk. Oh, yeah, there was the 187, a 182 built to the Cardinal design; and the 327, which was a baby Skymaster. The problem there was that nobody gave much of a hang about either one of the designs they were based on."

Cessna's 1971 XMC (Experimental Magic Carpet) single-engine pusher, a prototype that was "junked."

"Well, I'll bet Beech never made as many mistakes," someone volunteered.

"Not quite as many," Joe said. "Their PD 290—that was a King Air 200 with JT-15D turbojets on the wings in place of the turboprops—was sort of a test bed to see if they really wanted to build a jet. It convinced them that they'd rather buy someone else's headaches than have their own.

"Then they decided in the late '70s that a pressurized single was the coming thing, so they began fooling around with a T-tail Bonanza design called the T36TC. But the piston market began to fail, so they put all their efforts into a turbine-powered single, the 38P Lightning. And we know the rest of the story. There's a lot more of 'em, but those are the highlights."

"You can't forget the Cessna helicopter," we suggested.

There was a reverent pause, as if we were corporately searching for the correct words. Uninspired, no one spoke for a few seconds.

"Gee, I never realized how many designs they built," the youngster commented. "It's a real shame that all that time and money was wasted, and nobody got any good out of it."

"Oh, it wasn't wasted," Joe said as he lit a particularly offensive El Offal cigar. "The scrap dealers of Wichita are among the richest in the country." ✈

Making Aviation Art With a Nikon, a B-25, and "Liquid Light"

WICHITA, Kansas—You have to get up pretty early in the morning to get ahead of Paul Bowen. As a matter of fact, late risers may miss the top-rated aviation photographer, because his favorite shooting time is just before sunrise.

You've seen and undoubtedly admired one of Paul's 300 covers for *Flying*, *Canadian Aviation*, *Flight International* and other publications. Or you may have seen the corporate brochures of (alphabetically) Astra, Beech, Bell, Canadair, Cessna, Falcon, Gulfstream, Piper, or Sikorsky. There are not very many—if any—photographers who can boast of working for virtually all of the competitors in the market.

If you're looking for a realistic, evenly-lighted three-view photo of an airplane on which you can count the rivets, don't call Bowen. His work leans more toward impressionism. Many of Paul's scenes are head-on or from-above shots of the airplane in front of striking backgrounds that consist of clouds or distinctive terrain, often shot with low and dramatic light levels. Perhaps his most famous is also one of his earliest: a head-on close-up of a Citation climbing sharply from a peninsula runway at Fort Bragg, NC. The latest variation was the March 1992 cover of *Flying* — a Citation VI climbing through a Lake Tahoe fog bank with a trail of curling wingtip vortices in the clouds behind the airplane's flight path.

Even the most accomplished photographer is apt to look at a Paul Bowen photograph and say to himself, "I wonder how he did that?"

One answer is Paul's favorite shooting platform. It's Tallmantz Aviation's converted North American B-25 — an airplane fast enough to keep up with most corporate jets — and most of the photos are taken with him literally hanging out of the airplane.

According to Paul, there are three shooting positions in the airplane. "We use the wrap-around glass nose when we're flying on the other airplane and don't have to give any hand signals," he explained. "When the other plane is flying on us and we are looking back at him, we either shoot from the waist position behind the bomb bay doors where there is a removable 2 x 3-foot window, or from the tail gunner position. The tail sticks out past the vertical stabilizers, so when I'm back there with the cone removed, I'm in the open." He shoots about 80 percent of his work with two 35mm Nikons equipped with 105mm and 80-200mm lenses.

Paul usually gets the bomber and the subject airplane into the air about 35 minutes before sunrise and begins shooting before the sun comes up.

"At that hour there is a very low light, a soft light. It's beautiful! When the sun does come up, we have about 30 minutes of gorgeous light." Looking down from above, he said, the light is flat on the side of the airplane, while the ground remains dark, and since the exposure is set for the aircraft, the background appears even darker and the airplane really stands out. "I call it 'liquid light.' It gives a liquid look to the aircraft, like you just poured Crisco on it."

In a new venture named Avart, Paul has chosen six of his most popular and striking images and is producing them on 24" x 30" bordered posters, and fold-over note cards.

In addition to the two aforementioned Citation photos, other choices include a Beech Starship over Bryce Canyon, a Beechjet 400 over the California coast, a Learjet 35 over the Golden Gate Bridge, and a surreal solarized print of the Stealth Fighter. Prints ($25 each, 3 for $65 and 5 for $90, plus shipping and handling) are on heavy stock with a metallic ink border and protective varnish coating. The 5" x 7" note cards come 12 to a box (2 of each subject or 12 of one for $15 plus s&h) with envelopes, and all can be ordered by telephone at (800) 697-2580, 24 hours a day.

Paul Bowen's photos transcend the realm of just being airplane pictures; they are art by any definition — especially by the resident art critic at our house. Paul has, it has been decided, captured such a perfect blend of color, texture and line in his Beechjet photo that it can share wall space with prints by Georgia O'Keefe and Tomchuk.

I still wonder how he did that? ✈

The Fall and Rise of Business in the Air Capital
February 1993

WICHITA, Kansas—We "gadded" up to the air capital last week to visit some friends, do some family business, and visit with some airplane folks, the latter an attempt to enlighten faithful readers and generate bookwork for the IRS.

En route we had intended to stop in Ponca City, OK and jaw with the Kestrel Aircraft Company, which is proposing a seminal Cessna 172-looking composite single. But alas, it seems that not only is the keel not laid for the airplane, but the company is in the throes of moving itself aways southwest of OKC to Chickasha. So, it will doubtless be awhile before any interesting aircraft details are available.

We rolled into Wichita in the midst of one of the city's patented horizontal blizzards and visited Cessna's new Citation Customer Center. If you haven't been to that particular venue since the days of yore, be prepared to be dazzled. No more middle class, blue-collar company. This world headquarters is an ultra-modern, expensive-but-tastefully-decorated palace of commerce with lounges and meeting rooms, electronic and computer programs, and specialists who are all dedicated to selling the Citation, which they did 102 times in 1992.

The new entry-level ($2.62 million) CitationJet, which premiered at the 1989 NBAA, received certification in record time in October of 1992. Cessna spokesman Dean Humphrey said that serial number 2, the first production airplane, is getting ready to go on a demo tour, while number 3 is being used to train in-house pilots. He added that number 5 and 7 will be the first customer airplanes, and he expects them to be delivered this month. Production is sold out through mid-1994, and the company projects deliveries of about 50 units this calendar year.

At the other end of the scale, Humphrey says orders for the almost-$13 million Citation X "are in the double digits," and the aircraft is expected to fly in September.

But not all is well in Doo-Dah. While Cessna and Learjet are expecting to increase their employment in '93 by 400 and 100 respectively, they probably won't have any trouble finding the people. Beech will reportedly lay off 325 employees this quarter from the Wichita operation, plus another 50 from Salina. Piaggio slashed its Wichita fuselage production by 50 percent and a couple of dozen people, and Boeing's announced cutback of 28,000 jobs company-wide will mean the loss of 6,000 jobs at the Wichita Division in 1993, and another 1,000 in 1994.

"There's a phenomenon going on surrounding the layoffs at Boeing," said Dave Higdon, aviation editor at the *Wichita Eagle*. "Groups are taking action. The Governor has created a task force, Boeing is studying how to ease the pressure on those who are laid off, and Congress is working on a bill to extend unemployment benefits. This has happened here before, but it always took weeks and months. Now, industry sees that if it wants to recover, it has to do it right now."

It seems the Peerless Princess of the Plains has always had a feast-or-famine economy, and when general aviation or commercial production slumps, everyone turns to defense contracts. But about the only defense contract around these days is the Joint Primary Aircraft Training System (JPATS), a $3 billion nut for which every company in town (and a bigger number of out-of-towners) is vying, but which only one will get. Wichita is a survivor, though. We got the word from one of the natives, a veteran who started his aviation career sewing fabric to the skeletons of the Beech Model 17 when they were the cat's meow.

"Do you think the industry will survive?" One asked over a cinnamon roll at the Daylight Donut Shop where Cessna Chairman Russ Meyer stops occasionally.

"Does Raggedy Ann have cloth lips?" he countered. ✈

Buyers May be Looking For Antithetic Benefits

IRVING, Texas — The young woman was eyeing the hopelessly antiquated, first-generation 1982 model IBM PC Jr. that we had displayed at the garage sale.

"Only 128 kilobytes, huh? Can it be expanded?" she asked. We shook our heads no. "Are there a lot of programs available?"

"No ma'am," we answered, adding, "about all it's good for is word processing — letters and stuff."

"Good. I'll take it. How much do you want for it?"

I love that lady! She wanted the unit for the antithesis of the market's intentions. It's darned hard to find anything computerish that just writes letters and stuff, which is about all of us Great Unwashed do anyway. Computer companies tend to tell you all the magical tricks their product can turn (its features) but very few things it can do for the user (its benefits).

Advertising people know about the power of benefits, but their clients usually want to make sure none of the hardware is missed. There is a tendency for many manufacturers to rely on features to sell what is built rather than to build what sells. Airplane people are no exception.

"This industry was absolutely obsessed with performance numbers in the past," observed Bill Monroe, the new president of Aerospatiale General Aviation. "You say to somebody, 'If you buy a Trinidad and it goes 160 knots, you'll be able to go from Dallas to New Orleans in two and one-half hours. But if you go in a TB-200, it will take you two hours and 50 minutes.'

"Twenty minutes? For what? What we're finding today is that buyers of our products are less concerned with performance — although it's important — but they tend to evaluate things in real terms."

Of course! While we've always wondered about the style the kite factories employ to advertise their aluminum *wunderfleugen*, we have nonetheless always given buyers credit for necessarily choosing an airplane based on its intended use — even if that use was ego-fulfillment.

We have been exposed recently to several of what the economics experts naively term the "new-age" type of buyer:

• A pipeline company purchased three Cessna 182RGs for use in patrolling its 5,274-mile route. Our assumption was that patrollers prefer slower aircraft, except for occasional dead-head flights.

"The speed capability is there," explained the operation's chief pilot, "but when you operate (a faster airplane) at lower speeds you have a lower fuel flow, and as many hours as these airplanes fly (160 per month), if you can improve your fuel performance by a half-gallon an hour, you're saving money in the long run."

• The manager of a metropolitan utility company's flight department explained how they chose an airplane to replace their aging King Airs in anticipation of operating more than 700 hours per year apiece: "Most of our flights are (in the surrounding states), so we couldn't use a real fast airplane because the TCA holds you down in speed and altitude going in and out of here. We looked at the criteria and said if we're going to operate aircraft for 15 years, perhaps we ought to buy one that was built to standards that would last that long under heavy use. We felt that Part 25 better met our needs and that all went together in our decision to buy a Citation V."

• Another operator bought a Lear 25 because of its useful load and range.

"We have our own fuel farm," he said, explaining that his fuel cost was about 85 cents a gallon. "The Lear has the ability to haul a load after you top it off — and when you're paying $2.20 a gallon on the road, it makes a big difference."

These three professional operators bought aircraft for three specific operational profiles that probably don't appear in any manufacturer's or dealer's master marketing plans. These three aircraft include: **1)** a slow, retractable single, **2)** a low-speed, low-altitude jet, and **3)** one that thinks it's a tanker.

"I think buyers today are much more practical," Monroe concluded. "Instead of being preoccupied with bragging rights in the hangar, the actual specific numbers are less important than they used to be."

This is quite an accomplishment, the world and yrs trly in agreement. It also marks the first time we have been included in a group termed "new-age." ✈

5.

Places We've Been...

Our first tale proves that truth is often funnier, if not stranger, than fiction. In 1990, Tom Casey attempted to set a record by flying around the world in a floatplane, landing only on water. In a Cessna 206, he would try to break the record of 175 days, set in 1924 by a Douglass World Cruiser. Who'd have thought things would go so awry?

Around the World in 180 Days, More or Less

May 1989

ST. PAUL, Minnesota — Our rambling a couple of weeks ago took us to South St. Paul, Minnesota, where Tom Casey's floatplane, *Liberty II*, was being readied for its round-the-world trip. Casey and Liberty II will attempt to break the long-standing record of 175 days, set in 1924 by a Douglass World Cruiser.

The primary sponsor is the Phillips 66 Company. We had arranged to meet with Casey and Jack Hammond, Phillips' manager of aviation sales. Jack flew up from Bartlesville in his 310, and we arrived a day earlier on the "great silver bird" and the red Avis at Richard E. Fleming Field, a general aviation airport of the finest tradition located just a mile or so from the Mississippi River. The airplane was at Wipaire, Inc., an FBO and purveyor of floats.

Now we've been around a lot of airplanes in our day, but we had to admit that where we're from, airplanes with boats stuck to their undersides are as scarce as grass around a cow lick. But judging from the number in and around South St. Paul, they're as common as thermal underwear in the Land of a Thousand Ponds.

Robert "Call me Wip" Wippinger is the one that lends part of his name and all of his expertise to the business. And what a business it is! Beavers, Caravans, 185s and 206s all over the place, all on Wipaire floats, some with wheels, some without. The shop on the airport, where part of Wip's 25-man crew was working on Casey's Cessna 206, is one of those wax-and-polish-the-concrete-floor operations in a couple of 1940s vintage Quonset hangars. Wipaire also leases several other hangars, and is constructing a new building that is destined to be the company's state-of-the-art, EPA-approved paint shop.

When we were there, mechanics were pulling the steel cylinders off Casey's brand-new IO-550 engine so they could be shipped to another of the flight's sponsors, Engine Components, Inc. (ECI) in San Antonio, Texas. ECI would work their magic on the cylinders with the Cermicrome process, which embeds silicon carbide in hard chrome, protecting the engine from rust and reducing oil consumption to virtually nothing, Casey explained.

June 1990

SEATTLE, Washington — We "gadded" here for Casey's bon voyage party. While in the neighborhood, we visited the Museum of Flight at Boeing Field. Whooee! It's as neat as they keep saying it is — well worth a visit or two to explore the nooks and crannies. Many of the aircraft are different than seen in the rest of the country because of the type of flying that's done in the Northwest.

The morning Casey left on his record flight, yrs trly, being a member of the support team, was charged with making sure Casey and his 206 got from where it overnighted at Benair Aviation on Renton Municipal, up to Sand Point. From there Casey would officially commence the flight, following a 9 a.m. ceremony staged for the benefit of the assembled local and national media.

We got to the airport about 7:30, at the same time as Casey; he hadn't yet filled the airplane with fuel — 200+ gallons — nor packed any of his survival gear. A sense of foreboding crept into our mind. The man had been planning this trip for,

Around-the-world pilot Tom Casey sits by his Cessna 206 before leaving Seattle on his epic adventure.

literally, months, and his sole luggage was one duffel bag. With some sense of panic, we helped him accomplish the aforementioned and he had the 206 carried out to the dock where we launched it and climbed aboard for the short ten-mile hop. Casey started the engine and we blasted across the lake like a whale. Fifteen minutes later, the consensus among pilot and honorary crew was that no amount of coaxing could convince this airplane to fly, let alone taxi at a speed smart enough to get on the step.

"Gotta offload some fuel," Casey muttered as he keyed the mike and called the fuel truck back to the shore.

"Hey," we said nobly, "that will take too long, and you don't want to be late for your press conference, so offload us!"

After some discussion, he concurred and left us to watch his mile-long takeoff run across the water, at which point we called a cab for the trip across town.

When the taxi arrived we somehow were not surprised to discover it was an ancient seven-cylinder Chevy station wagon driven by a bearded and tattooed fugitive from a Cheech and Chong movie. We would have been less frightened in the overloaded Cessna.

Meanwhile, Casey had landed at Sand Point and impatiently posed for pictures and gave a speech. Then he jumped in the cockpit, started the engine and hit the throttle. It coughed and died, and while he was attempting a restart, the Cessna drifted into a dock with a tinny clang. No damage, but an inauspicious beginning.

When we returned to the hotel that afternoon, CNN was running its promised publicity on the flight. At least the dock-bumping sequence assured us of the comic relief spot at 55 past the hour all day long.

Casey had intended to fly north to Alaska and then make a left turn into Soviet airspace. But when he left, he didn't have clearance — another forgotten detail. Three days after arriving in Alaska, he still hadn't made the A list, so he decided to turn around, fly east across the continental U. S. and then through western Europe, hence, hopefully through the USSR. When permission was again withheld, he opted for the Southern Route, through the Mid-east and under Asia.

On August 28 Casey strained a muscle in his back while loading fuel in Cairo. When the pain started to affect his performance, he checked himself into the hospital at his next scheduled stop, which happened to be in Jeddah, Saudi Arabia.

How could he know that the Gulf War would begin the next morning?

After six weeks in bed Casey returned to the air, skirting around battle zones and flying across the Indian Ocean and to a base in northern Japan. Still denied entrance to Russia, he decided to make the 1,600 mile hop to the Aleutian Islands non-stop, although the distance was beyond the theoretical range of his airplane. He made it with quarts to spare, but the next day he blew his engine on takeoff and had to sit and wait for another powerplant to be shipped from Teledyne Continental.

Casey finally arrived home in Seattle amid less fanfare than accompanied his departure, with the Douglas World Cruiser record still standing. ✈

Visiting the Folk and Food of New Orleans

NEW ORLEANS, Louisiana — We had to fly to The Queen City recently for a few days to do some editorial-type work in preparation for this year's NBAA Convention. Another purpose of the trip was to obtain information and experiences for the purpose of writing a "destinations" travel article.

Now usually when we do a travel piece, we recommend the better and/or more modest-priced restaurants where the best cuisine/value per mouthful can be received. However, in New Orleans, Baton Rouge and every place in-between, it's practically impossible to get bad food. Louisiana grub is so good that one of the best meals we had — a shrimp Po-Boy sandwich for $4.95 — was at an airport restaurant!

We visited Lakefront Airport, site of the NBAA static display, and its director John Maloney. John is a New England Irishman who came to New Orleans after retiring as a Navy captain. John showed us around the terminal building, which is a marvelous example of the Art Deco architecture which has been hidden under neo-sixties concrete panels. If you know where to look, and John did, you can find WPA-era murals and bias relief sculptures depicting the history of aviation as it was known in the 1930s.

Lakefront has one airport-owned fuel farm to feed its five FBOs, and it's a computerized marvel at which refuelers can fill up day or night, jet or avgas. In addition, Lakefront may be the only airport in the country that is growing its own new ground. Perched on the edge of huge Lake Ponchatrain, the property is continually eaten away by the water, but operations to reclaim the land have been underway for several years. Of course, you can't drain anything in New Orleans because it's at sea level (even the bathtubs are elevated — honest!), so workers use a "wick" to sponge moisture out of the topsoil (which is referred to as coffee grounds). New dirt is added to the soggy soil, and its weight squeezes water out.

Flying over to International, we noticed on the chart that the airport, at four feet MSL, is somewhat lower than Lakefront. FBO Patrick Dugan of General Aviation Corporation claimed that his ramp was nine feet below sea level.

We opted to "Hertz it" over to Baton Rouge, where we talked with a couple of corporate flight departments and a charter operator. There were two reasons why we chose driving over flying: 1) so we could sample the Andouille sausage made in La Place, and stop at the various crawfish, gumbo and soft-shell crab establishments on the way, and 2) Baton Rouge's LSU is the alma mater of our co-pilot, best friend and spouse—who spent half a day poring over the phone book looking for an old classmate whose name she couldn't remember but would know when she saw it. Flying the 90-mile trip would have taken 45 minutes each way. Driving in the snack mode took three hours and twelve Rolaids®.

It isn't true that New Orleanites only eat and talk about eating, a native informed us. They also cook and compare recipes.

Bon apetit!   ✈

Ike's restored Columbine II *sparkles on the ramp at his hometown airport in Abilene, KS.*

What Would Ike's Centennial be Without Columbine II?

November 1990

ABILENE, Kansas — Blew up here (20 kt tailwind, as usual, when going south to north in the fall) for the conclusion of the city's year-long Eisenhower Centennial celebration.

One of the main reasons we came here was to see the just-finished restoration of *Columbine II*, the Lockheed Constellation Ike employed as *Air Force One* when he was commander in chief. Sitting majestically at Abilene Municipal Airport, authentically dripping oil on the ramp, the airplane was surrounded by a small force of Ryan and Vultee BTs and PTs, Stearmans, a Beech C-4 and Staggerwing, and T-6s. The Connie held an open house for thousands of visitors for three days, and did a Saturday twilight flyover at the Eisenhower Center to open an all-night vigil ceremony. On Sunday, an ecumenical church service on the grounds of the center was highlighted by the Reverand Billy Graham eulogizing his old friend, the former president.

An estimated 25,000 people flooded Ike's hometown for the festivities, and a Kansas trooper told us he had counted tags from 40 states. A group of veterans arrived on steam-engined "troop trains" from Kansas City, and several hundred mock troops with WWII vehicles and hardware encamped in Eisenhower Park. A railroad museum from Green Bay, WI even shipped the English-built *Dwight D. Eisenhower*, the streamlined locomotive and private cars Ike used in England during the war, for our viewing pleasure.

The Centennial ended Sunday evening with a laser show/pageant/fireworks display worthy of cities a hundred times the size of Abilene. As the music and drama built to the climax, literally hundreds of aerial displays erupted from behind the stage area, and the spectators, many of whom served with Ike over 45 years ago, cheered with patriotic fervor.

In the midst of the cheering, the voice of gospel singer Sandy Patty came over the sound system in the form of her unique rendition of the Star-Spangled Banner. At the same time, the fireworks erupted in even more spectacular displays, concluding with a two-minute frenzy of aerial bombs and shells.

If an Army recruiter had been there taking names, he could've had us all.

The trooper we spoke to said there was quite a number of law officers in town, but they had not had any major problems.

"Most of these people are from Middle America," he said. "They don't park where they're not supposed to park. They don't walk on the flowers."

Sounds like Oshkosh.

Harry Oliver and Mel Christler own *Columbine II*, which was purchased along with four other Connies in 1970 by Christler for use as aerial tankers. But *Columbine II's* origin wasn't known until 1980. In the meantime, the famous Connie had been stored in Tucson and systematically dismantled for parts.

"I felt real bad about it," Christler said. "I tore it apart and I wanted it back together to take its rightful place in history."

He tried to interest the Air Force and others in restoration, but everyone took one look at it and said it would never fly again.

"There were no engines, no props...the tail had been bouncing off the ground for ten years," he said. "All the instruments were gone and the wiring was just cut off. The only things left were the basic fuselage and the wings."

Oliver, a Santa Fe, NM resident who has a ranch in Wyoming, had taken off the past year to work with others on the restoration. He and seven friends spent six days a week working on *Columbine II*.

The Connie was first used by Ike after his 1952 election, including a trip to Korea which he promised voters if he was elected. Designated *Air Force One* in January 1953, Ike named it *Columbine II* after the state flower of Colorado, Mamie Eisenhower's home state. *Columbine I*, another Connie, had been used by Ike in Europe during World War II.

Columbine II retained its *Air Force One* rank until November of 1953 when it was returned to the regular ranks of the Air Force. Its last government flight was April 1, 1968.

Thanks to Christler and Oliver, and many other good folks, another generation can share the Eisenhower years. ✈

Napping Off to Nappanee

NAPPANEE, Indiana — After two days and 3,000 miles encased in the aluminum tubes of MD-80s, 727s, and 737s, jetting from Dallas to Miami to Chicago, it was a pleasure to slip into the more leisurely pace of Nappanee, Indiana, a city of 5,500 located some 100 miles east of Chicago and south of South Bend.

Nappanee, while not a national tourist destination, has its own special attraction in Amish Acres, which is interesting enough to do a destinations article on as soon as our metabolism gets back to speed.

The Amish in Indiana are similar to other settlements of their faith around the country, eschewing motorized transportation, electricity, telephones and other modern contraptions, living the simple life of 150 years ago.

We wheeled into the Nappanee Municipal Airport to talk with James Boyer, manager of JB Air Service. Assisted by his daughter, Arveta Gates, Jim does maintenance and mechanicing along with running the FBO. As we talked, a flight of two — a Navion and a V35 Bonanza — arrived to take on fuel. The pilots were headed for Indianapolis out of the Chicagoland area and had stopped for some of Nappanee's $1.50 + tax 100 Low Lead.

"Before you leave, I should show you who got me interested in flying," Boyer said as he produced a handful of newspaper clippings. "I shouldn't leave my Dad out of it," he stated as he showed us articles about the flying grandmother of Goshen (IN), "but Mom was the one. I'm kinda proud of her; she's still flying.

"My folks moved in at the north end of the runway there the same year the airport moved to its present location," he said. "She got her license to fly in '47, so I kinda grew up with it. "

Returning to the business at hand, Boyer said the Nappanee hangars house about 15 aircraft. He insisted there was nothing very special about the airport — just a few Cessnas, an Ercoupe...and then he remembered the Fleet which a man had owned for 20 years, and in which he was finally getting a pilot's license...and a lady who owned a Stampe, a French design whose Renault engine had been so unreliable that it was being replaced by something more conventional.

Boyer, who has an A&P rating, services aircraft based at Nappanee as well as other airports, and he did 28 annual inspections last year. "Here's one I work on," he said as he pointed at the picture of a Piper Warrior owned by his mother, "but there's no question why she comes in," he added with a hearty laugh.

The airport has one 3,000-foot paved runway, and as Boyer showed us around the facility he pointed to the west end of the strip. "You see that cow path out there?"

We looked and saw a path worn in the green grass, bisecting the center of the runway.

"There's not a cow around, but there's three Amish brothers who run a woodworking shop in that house over there. We've got a pay phone on the ramp here, and it's their company telephone. They've worn a path using it. I even saw one of them using an AT&T credit card once."

While the Amish may have a patent on the simple life, visiting folks at a small country airport can give you a taste of that simple life, making the big cities with their jets, traffic jams, and TCAs look positively silly. ✈

Hooks Airport Arises From the Rubble

SPRING, Texas — David Wayne Hooks Memorial Airport is alive and well, even though its famous water runway hasn't seen a seaplane for years. The restaurant is open again, new hangars are going up, and this general aviation airport, located at the northern reaches of Houston, is looking prosperous.

A few years ago there was some doubt it would ever survive. The problem wasn't the creeping urban incursion that many suburban airports suffer from, nor the complaints of neighbors. It was a much more Texas thing — a tornado — which nearly spelled Hooks' doom.

Nearly every airplane parked at the field on that summer day in 1986 was damaged, along with most of the main hangars and outbuildings. Within the few seconds it took for the twister to rumble through, walls fell in and roofs collapsed on million-dollar jets and turboprops, and on employees' cars. No lives were lost on the airport, although there was a fatality in a nearby mobile home park.

In the immediate aftermath, noble rebuilding plans abounded. But the combination of time and a souring economy eliminated some of the comeback fervor. Within two years or so, the airport was on the market. That's when J. S. Gill took an interest in the property and made an investment for its acquisition.

Meeting Gill's son Jaq, who runs the facility for the family company, tells a great deal about the diversity of modern Houston. Jaq is Indian — not the Texas kind, but the Asian kind. He is tall, dark, and beturbaned, and he speaks with an impeccably crisp and correct Oxford accent that reveals the home of his childhood. The Gill family emigrated to London from India in the early 1950s and invested in real estate. Mr. Gill, Sr. got the Hooks venture rolling in Texas while Jaq finished his Master's Degree at George Washington University. Mr. Gill stayed for another six months, and then turned management over to his son.

"Probably, he feels that as I got my education in America — which is where most of his children want to live — this would be more suited for me," Jaq reckons.

Even though Jaq was not schooled in airport management, he is savvy in business, and the careful building and rebuilding at Hooks has already produced results.

"The airport had not been run as professionally as people would have liked," Jaq said. "The late Mr. Hooks lost interest; he had been letting it tick along without doing anything to it. When we took it over, we put a substantial amount of funds into it — resurfacing the runway, opening the restaurant, starting a rental car business — and generally tried to run things in a more professional manner."

Hooks is a beehive of training activity, with four fixed-wing and two helicopter flight schools, an A&P school, and 100 percent hangar occupancy. Gill estimates that between 350 and 400 aircraft are based there. He is planning on enclosing some of the existing hangars, enough to house an additional 100 aircraft.

Like the mythical Phoenix, Hooks has risen from its own rubble, and as a local indicator of general aviation activity, it gives Houston a great deal of hope.   ✈

Flying "The Fourteeners" in South Central Colorado

SALIDA, Colorado — Even catching your breath at this 7,489-foot-high airport can be quite a chase for a flatlander, but there are 15 other airports in the state that are even higher.

When we visited Salida Air Service, owner Wil Atkinson was helping a student plan a cross-country to the highest airport. Leadville, 50 miles north of Salida and 2,500 feet higher, is the closest airport to the sun on the North American continent.

While the name of this South Central Colorado town some 50 miles west of Cannon City means "exit" in Spanish, it's really an entrance to the rugged part of the Rocky Mountains. Situated on the Arkansas River, Salida is a center for white-water rafting, hiking, and hunting, while serving as a gateway to Aspen and other ski areas.

"We use 172s for training," Atkinson said. "A 150 or a 152 might cut it, but for cross-countries, it's a little marginal."

Marginal indeed! With a host of what the locals call "The Fourteeners" — mountains 14,000 feet or higher — both of those aircraft could be at their service ceiling before they clear the peaks if some smart preflight figuring was not done. Of course, Atkinson's students never get to fly in fat air, so they wouldn't know the difference, would they?

The student had diligently figured his density altitude at about 10,500 feet on the 83-degree day, which meant that his takeoff run would be extra long. But he also knew the runway sloped downhill 200 feet in the direction he was taking off.

"Students are pretty savvy about the weather here," Atkinson said. "It's pretty consistent. During the summer you normally get pretty nice mornings and in the afternoon there is a cloud buildup and thunderstorms."

Besides training, Atkinson and his partner, Joyce Hanagan, also run the Unicom and fuel pumps while taking on charter, sightseeing and other commercial work. When we visited, they were looking forward to the impending arrival of a 210 to make the trips to Denver and Colorado Springs easier and faster.

Hanagan said the FBO also has some out-of-town customers who rent Salida Air Service aircraft for their own touring. Checkout requires the normal demonstration of proficiency plus a review of the special rules and techniques of mountain flying: "The airplane doesn't work well, so you have to figure other ways to get higher," she said.

For a person so versed in high-altitude flying, we were surprised to learn that Atkinson grew up in Wichita, Kansas. After a stint at Learjet, he moved to Colorado — "Because I always wanted to." — and worked for Martin Marietta in Denver for three years before going to Colorado Springs in 1982 with Digital Equipment Corporation.

Atkinson found the FBO at Salida through an advertisement, and he jumped at the opportunity to buy it. It was a decision he has never regretted.

It is easy to see why Wil Atkinson and Joyce Hanagan think they have found their niche. The pressures of big business seem not so important in the Rockies. The surroundings demand that the flatlanders and the big city people learn to slow down and smell the columbines. Once that is accomplished, you find yourself idly window shopping for a 4 x 4 and comfortable boots. Then you notice a particular plot of land that looks like it could use a log cabin on it.

Within a few days, the natives say, you get used to the thinner air — but they are careful to never mention that you will get back to normal. ✈

Name-Dropping Requires the Correct Articulation

We intended to file the next column from *General Aviation News & Flyer's* European office (a rented Peugeot parked on the *Rue de Rivoli*), but often the only way to work a trip like this into a conversation is to just blurt it out.

"Yeah, we're going to Paris next week," we said in a markedly unsubtle manner to a friend from Florida who was in town. "Paris, Texas?" he countered in a move designed to deflate the importance of the statement.

"The other one," we replied, smiling benignly. "If you were a Texan, you'd know that when you're talking about Paris, Texas, you refer to it as 'ParisTexas.' The foreign one is always called by just its front name." (That reminds me of the following saying: Never ask a fella if he's from Texas; if he is, he'll tell you without having to be asked, and if he ain't, it might embarrass him.)

Actually, we'll be headed for Toulouse, France to ride along on the ferry flight of a new ATR-42. The plane is coming to the U.S. via Iceland and Labrador.

• • •

Speaking of famous places, we got our semi-annual packet of information last week from Chuck Morrow of Ram Aircraft Corporation. The company, founded by Jack Riley, Jr., is located in Waco, Texas and specializes in performance modifications.

We've been to Ram a couple of times in recent years, but we always tell Chuck the reason we don't visit more often is that we can't remember how to get there (Waco is about 100 miles south of us — too far to drive, too short to fly).

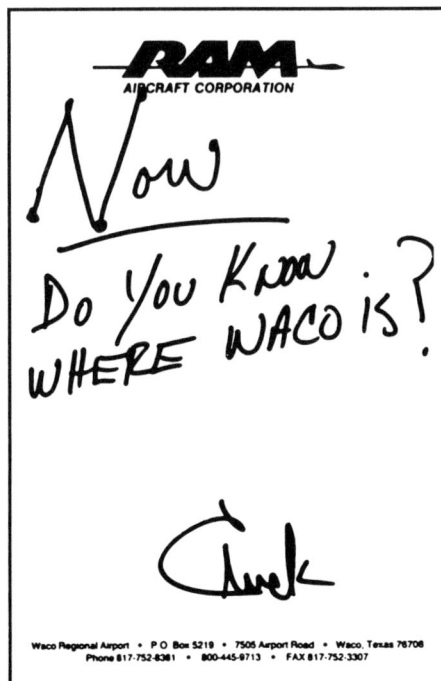

RAM
AIRCRAFT CORPORATION

Now

Do You Know
Where WACO is?

Chuck

Waco Regional Airport • P.O. Box 5219 • 7505 Airport Road • Waco, Texas 76708
Phone 817-752-8381 • 800-445-9713 • FAX 817-752-3307

Waco, also home of the infamous Branch Davidian standoff, has recently been in the news. So, in a display of last-wordsmanship, Chuck attached a note to the material he sent me (see left).

• • •

Bill Neale, a nationally known Dallas automotive artist who has also done some aviation illustration in his time, was telling us what happened on a recent trip to Colorado. He had stopped in a cafe and ordered iced tea, the Texas state drink.

"When the waitress served me something red in a glass, I asked 'What's this?' and she said it was *Asti Spumonti*. I told her I didn't order *Asti*," Bill said in his best Texas accent, "I ordered **Ahced Tay!**"

It reminds us of the time we

stopped in an Oklahoma airport restaurant a few years ago and asked what kind of pie they had.

"Apple, cherry and diet nut," the waitress drawled.

"Diet nut?" we asked, puzzled. "What's in it?"

"Diets and nuts," she answered in disbelief of our simple mindedness. "You know — diets, those things that grow on palm trees." (Editor's note: For the botanically impaired, like me, *dates* are the edible fruit of date palm trees. —Greg Bayer) ✈

Postcard From Another Bizarre Location

REYKJAVIK, Iceland—Sitting in our room at the Hotel Loftledir overlooking the ramp and spare landscape on this delightful island, it occurred to yrs trly that this may be the most unusual venue from which it has been our pleasure to file a "Gadding With GAN" column. It had been almost 35 years since we had been treated to a visit to this exceptional country, and we were anxious for the experience.

The day started in Toulouse, France, where we boarded an ATR (Avions Transport Regionale) 42 painted in American Eagle livery. Some six hours and 1,600 nautical miles later, we paused here in Reykjavik on the delivery flight which would ultimately take us to Albany, New York. There the 44-passenger propjet built by the Aerospatiale-Alenia combine would be outfitted for commuter work and go on-line virtually hours after our arrival.

Toulouse, a city of 300,000 in Southern France, could be compared to Wichita (Beech, Cessna, Lear), or Renton, WA (Boeing) if the French were of a mind to compare their cities with ours, which they are not.

As home to Aerospatiale's Airbus and ATR operations — in addition to divisions of Dassault, Matra, Hohr, and others—a visit revealed more large, fat airliners than we had seen in years. These airliners included a "Guppy," the converted Boeing C-97 specially modified to carry Airbus fuselage sections and wings in its bloated interior.

Also extant at the Aerospatiale facility is a real live *Concorde*. It has been on permanent display since the day some workman reportedly filled its hydraulic reservoirs with a fluid that rendered all its systems useless. It looked smallish next to some of its later, larger cousins.

Aerospatiale, of course, is that amalgamation of virtually every French aircraft manufacturer since Bleriot, and a trip around the perimeter of the airport revealed a bone yard of historic French prototypes, and a DC-3.

The only hitch in our departure day had been that we got up one hour late. It seems that daylight savings time had come to the country a week or so earlier, and no one had bothered to reset the clock in the computer that makes wake-up calls.

"I am sorry, Monsieur; it is the computer. It is not yet set, so, you see," the hotel clerk said with a Gaulic shrug, "it is not my fault."

It was better explained by our contact at Aerospatiale: "Oh, you know," she said with a similar hunched-shoulder, hands-turned-up posture, "we are French."

So it was with culture shock that we got off the aircraft in Iceland to find efficient and timely service and pristine surroundings.

The traffic at Reykjavik is sparse, and virtually all intercontinental. Making Iceland from the UK is not all that difficult, but going west, the next available fuel is in Greenland, then Labrador. It was surprising to see several Cessna 152s on the ramp at the FBO's flight training operation. We were assured they had been ferried from the North American continent.

Tomorrow we leave for Goose Bay, Labrador and the United States. The next day we'll be back home and into the day-do-day, but it will be hard to find a better place than this from which to correspond.

There may, however, be a less expensive place. We just got the bill for faxing this to Tacoma, WA — 1,460 kronur ($21.39). ✈

Never Ask if Someone Can Fly an Airplane — Ask How

ATLANTA, Georgia — It was easy to catch up with student David West as he walked toward the airplane parked on the ramp in front of Epps Air Service at DeKalb Peachtree Airport.

Easy because all we had to do was carry a cumbersome camera bag, while David had to handle his gear plus support himself with two walking canes.

David, from Newcastle upon Tyne, England, is one of three handicapped Britons who are taking private pilot flight training at Epps under financial sponsorship of the RAF Benevolent Fund (RAFBF). While the others are wheelchair bound, David has a progressive arthritis, the result of which is a rigid spine and neck, and can walk with the help of two canes. Nonetheless, he was preparing for his short cross-country solo with the same fretful care all students exhibit, checking over every inch of the airplane.

Epps, a Piper dealer for years, uses Warriors IIs with various modifications to fit different physical conditions.

"The key to success is asking the right kind of questions," explained Chief Flight Instructor Clint Rodgers. "We never ask *if* someone can fly an airplane, we ask *how*. What do we have to do to make it possible for them to fly?"

West showed us a couple of ingenious methods developed by the Epps flight training staff for his program.

While wheelchairs are low enough to allow students to check fuel drains on the low-wing aircraft, David couldn't operate at that level. So the Epps staff simply glued the fuel checker to the end of a broomstick. In addition to being able to perform the fuel draining exercise, David also has learned to manipulate tie-down ropes with the appliance.

And the day we visited, a mechanic had glued clips to the backs of a pair of concave mirrors. By fitting one to each side of the glare shield David could check the view to the side of, and behind, the cockpit.

Rodgers teaches all the instructors to fly with the same handicap condition as the person they're teaching.

"If they (the instructors) are flying with a paraplegic, I require them to fly without ever putting their feet on anything. When we get into the airplane, we don't have anything at our disposal that they (the handicapped students) don't have — they have to have confidence that the system works."

The training program, which has produced more than 60 students, is supported through the RAFBF by Jordan's English-educated King Hussein. The king annually funds six scholarships in memory of Sir Douglas Bader, a celebrated pilot who just happened to be handicapped. Bader lost his legs in a low-level aerobatic crash in 1931 and was forcibly retired from the RAF. In 1939, after a bitter struggle against the bureaucracy, he was allowed to serve again and eventually took over the Duxford Wing during the Battle of Britain.

Ironically, while the program has an undeniable value as an esteem-builder, once students have earned their U.S. licenses and return home, they are not recognized as bona-fide PIC pilots in the United Kingdom because of their physical limitations.

"Each International Civil Aviation Organization (ICAO) member country is supposed to recognize licenses issued by all the others," Rodgers said. "The problem is that when the students go back to England, they'll be flying UK-certified aircraft with a U.S. certificate, and that just doesn't wash."

He added that if an Englishman came here, he could easily get a U.S. certificate based on his English license.

"There are a couple of young ladies (former Epps students) who are taking on the CAA. The BBC has agreed to do a program and invite one of these outspoken people, and she'll make it a national issue. The CAA is not very happy with us right now."

However, Dennis Middleton, David West's instructor, must be happy with his student's progress. This is evident from his sensitive demeanor and encouraging words shouted as West closed the cockpit door prior to departing on his short cross-country solo.

"Hey! Good luck, and remember: Don't bend my airplane!"   ✈

Plans for Irrevocable Retirement Can Go Awry in the Mountains

PAGOSA SPRINGS, Colorado—When we "gadded" to Southwest Colorado in mid-September, we traded density altitude for the real thing. At 7,700 feet, Stevens Field is way down on Colorado's list of top ten highest airports.

We were in town along with a neighbor to investigate the possibility of permanently escaping North Texas summers by purchasing a quaint little cabin in the woods. However, the fact that there are 27 real estate agencies in this quiet little town of 3,000 or so would tend to indicate that they know whereof we came.

At one of the aspiring properties that backed up to the airport, we noticed a Waco being towed out of its nest, so we hot-footed it over to Stevens Field to inquire of its origin.

Stevens' newest runway, a 1.06-mile ribbon of asphalt, parallels its older, shorter counterpart, which does duty nowadays as a taxiway. That is where we found the red, white and blue biplane (a 1940 UPF-7), and its pristine Cessna 195 hangar-mate.

Larry Bartlett greeted us as we walked into the hangar, and we seemed

*The "retired" Larry Bartlett with his 1940 Waco UPF-7 in
Pagosa Springs, Colorado.*

somehow to already know each other. Turns out that Larry is a faithful reader of
General Aviation News & Flyer, and yrs trly remembered his Examiner's column
from the old days when "The Green Sheet" was published in Snyder, Texas.

"I retired from the Army in 1969, and until 1983 I had a flight school and air
taxi business in El Paso, and was an examiner and corporate pilot," Larry
recounted. "My wife and I used to come up here in the '70s on vacation, and then
when I retired, we decided to move here."

He really wanted to go to Alaska — he had spent eight years there — but
reasoned that Colorado's *Northern Exposure*-like ambiance was a more practical

compromise, and also closer to the grandkids.

Pagosa's new runway was finished five years ago, and Larry soon built the first of several hangars that now sit alongside the old strip. Besides providing a home for his airplanes, the space is used for activity in what the 66-year-old Bartlett calls his "third irrevocable retirement" That is, he now produces flying videos such as the best-selling "Flying the Alaska Highway."

"We've done six videos," Bartlett explained, "and Sporty's sells five of them. They do a tremendous job."

Checking on his computer, he calculated a total of about 10,000 tapes marketed, 3,000 of which are the Alaska video.

"The video business bought my Waco and the hangar," he added with a grin.

Currently, he is in the final phases of bringing out a new program, "Flying the Colorado Rockies," which he thinks should be on the market in a month or so.

"It's not a mountain flying tape *per se*," he said, "because Sparky Imeson has a good one. But it'll be a tour of the Rockies for flatland pilots who are afraid to fly in the mountains. A little bit of instruction, but primarily a tour, to mollify the wife or the husband about flying in this country."

Larry and his wife do most of the camera work from the 195, although obviously any shots of the Cessna flying over the scenery must be done by another crew.

Larry has owned the 195 since May of 1963, in which time he has flown the plane half of its total 6,000 hours. He purchased the three-place Jacobs 275-powered Waco three years ago to use for sightseeing, charter, and occasional aerobatic work, but soon after developed heart problems and had quadruple by-pass surgery. Although he got his medical reinstated eight months after the operation, he opted for the simpler qualification of a Third Class certificate.

"I've really got no basis to keep the Waco now that it isn't fun," he said. "I've got five people that are trying to buy it from me, but amazingly enough, my wife says keep it and play with it awhile!"

Some people just cannot stand the thought of not being involved in day-to-day business. Others handle retirement gracefully. Larry Bartlett seems to have found a level that satisfies both attitudes. ✈

Priester's 40-Year Odyssey in Business Aviation

WHEELING, IL — It must have been a dozen and a half years since we had "gadded" to Pal-Waukee Municipal in suburban Chicago to visit Priester Aviation. A great deal has changed during that time, including the ownership and the look of this venerable FBO. However, hangar flying is pretty much the same, and when we visited with Priester Aviation President Charlie Priester, we were able to talk a little about the history of the operation between "do you remember?" stories.

George J. Priester originally bought the 153-acre field in 1953 from Parks Aircraft. "There was no blacktop, no hangars, no electric runway lights," explained Charlie. "We used flare pots — filled them with kerosene, loaded 'em on the back of an old International truck, set 'em out on the runway where we thought the wind was going to blow all that night, and lit'em. Then we picked them up the next morning and started all over again.

Charlie says that although he likes to say that his Dad bought Pal-Waukee after conducting an extensive market study, the truth is that it was the only airport for sale at the time. And when it looked like jets were going to be the thing to fly, George and Charlie went to all the aircraft manufactures and did another quasi-scientific study to find out just how much runway would be enough to handle the new-fangled airplanes. When the number kept coming out at around 5,000 ft., the Priesters went looking for enough land to extend their 3,000 ft. strip. Four land deals and 100 acres later they added a strip of land large enough to build the runway, although the airport then as now is L-shaped.

The talk about visiting the jet factories spawned a story from Charlie: "Lear's sales manager is standing in the hangar one day and Bill's about ready to ink this doctor on an early Learjet, and the doctor looks at Lear and says, 'Now Bill, are you sure I can fly this jet?' Bill looks at him and says, 'Why doctor, if you can fly your Bonanza, you can fly this jet!' Lear walks away and the sales manager leans over to the doctor and says, 'You'd better be one **damned** good Bonanza pilot!' and Lear heard it and fired him."

George Priester, now a still-active 85 years old, had been an engineer on the Chicago Northwestern Railroad, as was his father before him. But he was also an aviator, learning to fly in 1928 (his license is No. 18394). When he started George J. Priester Aviation, Charlie said, his father recognized that aviation served business, and although nearly everybody in those years was in sales, Priester focused more on service. While larger business aircraft operators contributed to the majority of their profits over the years, the FBO tried not to ignore the smaller business aircraft users.

"When you think about it, it doesn't have to be General Motors to be corporate aviation," Charlie suggested. "The business user has more urgency (than the casual user), and they're not using discretionary income."

Priester was a long-time Cessna dealer, but Charlie admits that they did not get active in sales until the company premiered its Conquest turboprop.

In 1986, faced with the prospect of encroaching housing, annexation, and local zoning ("there was nothing we could do with approaches: we were really held hostage to what the local communities may elect to do"), the Priesters sold Pal-Waukee jointly to the Village of Wheeling and the City of Prospect Heights. "But," as Charlie is wont to say, "that's another whole story."

In 1991, the FBO changed hands.

"We decided that if the company was going to keep going, we would either have to invest a lot of money or find some people who have the same business philosophy." There were meetings with several major FBO chains, but Priester worried about the fate of his employees and a possible change in the character of the business.

"Then a friend of mine, Dick Ferris (former chairman of UAL, Inc., parent company of United Airlines), came in out of the blue," Charlie explained. "We sat down one Saturday morning and he made an offer from himself and Arnold

Palmer and we struck a deal before lunch." Charlie remained president, and became a partner a year later.

Today, Priester has 546,000 square feet of hangar space, making it possibly the largest wholly-owned single FBO operation in the country. There are approximately 300 aircraft on the field, and about 35 corporate operations, most with familiar names. Priester Aviation has 14 aircraft in its charter fleet, five of which are managed for owners. They include two piston-powered planes (a Beech 76 Duchess and a Cessna 414A), four turboprop aircraft (three King Airs and a Gulfstream I), and eight jets (a Citation I, a Learjet 25, three Learjet 35s, a Falcon 20, a Challenger, and a Gulfstream II).

George J. Priester had the right idea back in 1953 when he recognized that the airplane was tailor-made for business. Over the years, he gained the reputation of being stubborn, and may even have been termed a trouble maker. Factory salesmen often winced when they saw him coming.

"Yeah," mused Charlie, "but you didn't have any trouble figuring out what he meant. I give him credit. He may have been an agitator, but I prefer to think of him as an individual thinker." ✈

6.

...and People & Things We've Seen

"Auld Lang Syne" Rings True When You Run Into an Old Friend

IRVING, Texas — "Auld Lang Syne" (old long since), the once-a-year familiar lines penned by Bobby Burns, suddenly took on new meaning over the holidays when we ran into an acquaintance whom we hadn't seen since his retirement.

Jim Kemper, he of stork-like stature and gentle demeanor, was the fellow you always saw at Cessna's exhibit at Oshkosh and other venues, presiding over the display and visiting with the owners, former owners, and future owners (when the latter were considered at least a possibility). Jim and yrs trly matriculated at the University of Cessna at about the same time exactly a quarter-century ago, riding together like Don Quixote and Sancho Panza to challenge the windmills of corporate life.

What made Jim good at his job was his natural curiosity about everything and everybody. To that end, he is also a collector, a saver. You want to see an unopened pack of Lucky Strike Greens? They're in the drawer there. A Skyhawk brochure from 1965? In the filing cabinet. A souvenir sheet of unused, imperforate stamps from the 1933 Century of Progress Exposition in Chicago? Check the bulging stamp album.

While he was growing up in Dodge City, Jim collected autographs by writing to various luminaries, enclosing an SASE and a 3x5 card. He has lots of famous names in the collection — Herbert Hoover, Walt Disney, Wendell Wilkie — but his most prized is from Orville Wright, who sent Jim an autographed picture of the First Flight.

Since retiring, Jim and his wife Olive, also a pilot, have worked as volunteers for the National Park Service, manning information booths in parks throughout the country (including Alaska), and at the new History of Aviation museum at

Love Field in Dallas.

Auld Lang Syne indeed. Finding old friends may be as good as making new friends.

One of our newer friends is one of aviation's oldest friends, George Haddaway. For 44 years he published *Flight* magazine (until he sold it in 1974) and was general aviation's biggest promoter. George served as a voluntary advisor to six FAA administrators and received numerous accolades, including NBAA's Award for Meritorious Service to Aviation in 1976. He also received honors from the Air Force Association, Arnold Air Society, FAA, Aviation/Space Writers Association, American Association of Airport Executives, NATA, NAA, Daedalions, and more.

In his spare time he was founder and chairman of Wings of Hope, an airborne charity that furnishes aircraft for medical and logistical support to some of the world's neediest and most inaccessible countries.

While it's always a pleasure to visit George and look at the pictures on the wall of his den ("Say, is that Jimmy Doolittle posing with your kids when they were little, George? Oh, there's Chuck Yeager and you—is that your back yard? That's Walter Beech, and there's you with Arthur Godfrey, isn't it?"), you know that the probable price of admission is volunteerism in something.

While we haven't formally committed to his latest charitable project, after hearing about the prototype program and watching a videotape summary, it will be just a matter of time before we're immersed in it.

Centered in Denver and headed by an airline captain, this program involves a small group of potential dropouts — high school students with failing grades and minor scrapes with the constabulary. To head off a potential life of crime, and to shore up academic skills, the kids are enrolled in an aviation program.

Math skills are bolstered with real-life navigation and flight planning exercises. Physics and general science knowledge is increased by studying flight characteristics, meteorology and basic engineering. And communication and writing skills are sharpened with action/reaction exercises.

Still in its early stages, the program has a look of success about it. ✈

Air Force One and Baseball
April 1991

DALLAS, Texas — We recently went to visit Bob Via, manager of Citijet at Dallas Love Field and newly elevated chairman of the board at the National Air Transportation Association. As we pulled into the parking lot, we couldn't help but notice there was a lot of big equipment labeled "United States of America" sitting on the ramp. These aircraft had brought a host of congressmen to town for a memorial service for former senator John Tower.

At the same time, Air Force One was resting at Navy Dallas. President George Bush also attended the services, but his trip had originally been scheduled for a happier occasion: throwing out the first pitch of the season at the Texas Rangers' opening game, which was sold-out. The president's son, George W., happens to be a majority stockholder of the Rangers.

Two theories exist why some 40,000 people would subject themselves to stalled traffic, 30 percent higher ticket prices than last season, a herd of guard dogs, and a host of security checkpoints. Republicans insisted it was because the prez was there, while everyone else argued it was because Nolan Ryan was the starting pitcher.

Citijet's ramp was full of USA airplanes — a 707, a 727, and a C-130, which probably was for transporting support equipment. And Citijet's lobby was peopled with Air Force personnel and guys in three-piece suits wearing silvered sunglasses and talking into little black boxes they carried on their belts.

The FBO is used to traffic of that type. It handles a lot of VIP traffic and they all buy fuel — three million gallons of it last year! It seems to be accomplished smoothly and without trauma, all according to plan. That's a reflection of Via's calm attitude. You get the feeling that if a KC-135 taxied up and the pilot said, "Fill'er up," Bob's first question would be, "Cash or charge?"

But Via's stoicism is reserved solely for business. If you want to change the subject and get a reaction, bring up "real" flying or Brangus cattle. Bob, who was raised on a Midwest farm, is doing the Texas thing with a herd of registered Brahma-Angus crossbred cattle on a small ranch north of Dallas. Even though it's a hobby operation, you can bet that it's run with the same efficiency, and possibly even the same bottom line, as Citijet.

Meanwhile, at Arlington Stadium, the former captain of Yale's baseball team was doing his thing with the season's first pitch, throwing what some termed a "scud" pitch, a 48 m.p.h. (before the bounce) missile that may have put a new tax on the catcher's abilities. Unfortunately, full-time hero Nolan Ryan didn't do much better the rest of the evening, and the Rangers lost 5-4.

We stayed home and relied on the 10 o'clock news to organize the day's events. George Bush left during the fifth inning. Bob Via was probably at the ranch, telling his cows about all that had happened that day. ✈

Air Tractor Produces Four Tons of Honest Airplane Every Week

June 1991

OLNEY, Texas — On the way to the Oklahoma Aircraft Dealers Association auction in OKC a couple of weeks ago, we veered over to Olney, some 38 miles southwest of Wichita Falls (and south of Archer City, where Larry McMurty's "Last Picture Show" and "Texasville" were filmed) and home to Air Tractor, the world's largest agplane manufacturer.

While Air Tractor (AT) is no giant manufacturing complex, Olney is no metropolis either, and the two suit each other just fine. Leland Snow, president and CEO at AT, prefers the small-town atmosphere. Olney is where he started the original Snow Aeronautical after type certification of his S-2B design in 1958 (the one-off S-1 flew in 1953). Subsequent S-2 variants were built there, including the S-2R after Leland sold the company to Rockwell in 1965. When Rockwell moved production to Albany, Georgia in 1970, Leland stayed home and set up the current company with a new design, the AT-300, which first flew in September 1973.

Air Tractor Designer/President Leland Snow (left) poses with one of his turbine models, the AT-802 powered by a PT6A-67. The aircraft has an 800-gallon hopper and 16,000-lb. gross weight. Alongside Snow is the new owner, Jerry Dunson.

Meanwhile, Rockwell sold the agplane line to Ayres in '77, which still builds the S-2 line in Albany.

It's always like a breath of fresh air to get away from the accounting-driven factories with their multi-layered management bureaucracies and labor disputes and visit a place where airplanes are built with the customer in mind (instead of the marketing manager) and where cool heads prevail.

"We're building two airplanes a week," Snow related. "That means that every week we push four tons of airplanes out the door." He added that by the end of the month their half-year total will be 50. Last year, Air Tractor delivered 106 airplanes — no small feat for a company with only 113 employees, including Snow. And it's no component assembler, either; more than 80 percent of each model is fabricated on the premises.

"What we have in this area are people who are not afraid to work — they have a strong work ethic. We've had zero turnover this year; not a single person quit," he explained. "Last year only one quit, and that was because he'd applied for another job before he came here and it opened up."

The most surprising revelation we found during our visit was that the vast majority (upwards of 70 percent) of Air Tractors are the turbine-powered AT-402 and AT-502. This is a reversal of just a few years ago when better than two-thirds of the new airplanes flew out with standard agplane power, the Pratt & Whitney R-1340 radial.

Today's base price piston-engine model lists at $157,000, or $130,500 if you furnish the R-1340. An operator can also furnish his own PT6 with which to build a 400-gallon AT-402 or 500-gallon AT-502 for $165,500 to $176,500. Or a complete new-engine package is available for $369,500 to $379,500.

"I have to comment that in some cases the operator simply can't afford to get the higher cost of a new engine, so out of necessity they have to go to a used engine," Snow commented. "There's nothing wrong with that."

He added that about half of the turbine-powered models are built with customer-furnished engines. "We think that if a person goes ahead and buys a new engine today, that 10 years from now it will not only have held its value, it will probably have appreciated. Usually the first three or four years you're more concerned with making payments (than thinking of repairs), so we think that a new engine on a new agplane is a good investment."

And, Snow added, if an operator just cannot justify a turbine at this point, he can always put it on later (the piston-powered models can be converted to turbine power by any mechanic using the kit AT furnishes) simply by complying with a service letter and entering the switch in the airplane's logbook.

The newest project is the AT-802, a two-place Air Tractor that Snow has built to carry 800 gallons in its hopper. It has a 12,500 pound gross weight, a 1,424 shp PT6A-45, and its purpose is fire bombing.

"This airplane started from scratch as an air tanker. It was sized and configured purely to meet the requirements of at least equaling the performance and payload capabilities of the Grumman Tracker (powered by two Wright R-1820 radials)."

A big airplane, indeed, and it would have a big price if it weren't for the manufacturing magic the 113 Olneyites will perform.

"It will be an expensive airplane, compared to what we're used to selling. We're currently building and selling an 8,000-pound gross weight turboprop that sells for about $380,000, and that compares with a Cessna Caravan — also about 8,000 pounds with a similar engine — which sells for over a million dollars. We are very careful how we operate in order to sell (the AT-502) at that kind of price. Relatively speaking, the 802 is much more expensive. It will be in the neighborhood of $800,000 to $900,000 as an air tanker because it has a lot of very sophisticated equipment." The prototype is currently being leased by the State of California for use during the fire season.

All in all, a visit to Olney and Air Tractor reassures one that the free enterprise system is still alive, that simple, old-fashioned things like supply and demand, good value and the work ethic are one man's secret to continued success. ✈

About the Past, Present, & Future of the National Air & Space Museum

ADDISON, Texas — It's usually a small gathering, a bunch of the airplane boys getting together down in Arlington, Texas in some dark and smoky barbecue joint. It's a loose confederation of mostly military aircraft writers and buffs who get together once a month to study some interesting airplane. Their ersatz leader is Jay Miller, aviation author and publisher (Aero Fax).

But the November meeting was different. For one thing, it was at the Addison Airport, some 30 miles from the usual venue. For another thing, you could fly to this meeting. And if you did, you noticed when you taxied up there was hardly any place to park, what with an AT-6, a Stampe (pronounced "stomp") biplane and a Ryan trainer parked in front of David Strait's hangar. Strait is a jet warbird restorer with whom we shared a flight last spring in a Siai-Marchetti 221 jet trainer.

There already were 40 or 50 people there ooing and ahhing over the hardware when we arrived a half-hour early. There was the bright orange Bell X-1 Glamorous Glennis (actually, the mockup used in *The Right Stuff*), two Folland Gnats, a Saulnier Paris Jet, a Soko trainer, Strait's personal A-4, an LTV single engine turbine experimental model from some years ago, and a familiar-looking twin-tailed airplane parked in the corner — what Strait termed a "supersonic Ercoupe."

That kind of machinery tends to draw a crowd, but the reason everyone was there was to meet Walter Boyne, a former director of the National Air and Space Museum (NASM) in Washington, DC. Boyne retired from the USAF in '74 with the rank of colonel and more than 5,000 hours in a variety of aircraft including the B-47, B-50 and B-52. A prolific writer, he has produced a dozen or more books since leaving NASM, including *The Leading Edge*, *The Smithsonian Book of Flight* and a novel titled *The Wild Blue*. (There are more, but those are the only ones we have, now autographed, on our shelves.) His latest book, *The Power Behind the Wheel*, is about automobiles.

Boyne furnished an illustrated walk through the rather short history of the NASM, of which he was the first director, and discussed the political machinations that affected both its initiation and its ongoing operation.

"The word on the Mall (from Museum detractors) was that it might draw a million visitors in its first year and then settle back to half a million per year after that. The first year, it drew 10 million," Boyne recalled.

He went through all the agonies and triumphs of the building and opening of the facility with a collection of slides, pausing to make fond reminiscences about the museum's personnel.

"Museums have both curators and designers. Curators would like to cram everything they have in the museum with just enough room so that you can walk between things. If designers were in charge they would display just one aileron in a spotlight. So there has to be a balance."

The most popular exhibits in the NASM are the *Wright Flyer*, the *Spirit of St. Louis*, and the first human-powered aircraft, Boyne said.

"People will look at them and say, 'Yeah, I could fly that,' but when they get to a space capsule or the X-1, they say, 'Oh, I could never learn to do that!'"

Boyne's advice for aviation buffs visiting Washington, DC is to skip the NASM and go to Silver Hill, where aircraft are stored and restored. He estimated about 100,000 people visit there each year.

Boyne recounted how Silver Hill had grown virtually without congressional funding, and sometimes, even without that august group's knowledge (illustrating the philosophy that it's easier to get forgiveness than permission). In the mid-1980s, the restorers sought permission to build a display at Dulles Airport to house some of the exhibits that were too large for the Mall location, like the B-29 *Enola Gay*. The idea was defeated because of the political climate of the hour. So where does that leave the future of the National Air and Space Museum? If the trend continues, it will be in rockets and shuttles instead of airplanes. ✈

A Get-Acquainted Conversation With the Neighborhood Left-Seater

IRVING, Texas - Whilst motoring through the new part of town to which we moved last summer, we spotted a neighbor whom we had been wanting to meet. It was not so much Neighbor *per se*, but rather the sailplane we had often seen in his garage that we wanted to inspect. The plane's trailer top was popped and Neighbor was tinkering with some winglets, trying to figure out how to attach them and still get the whole assembly in the shrink-wrap enclosure.

After introducing ourselves, we found out Neighbor has been flying for Delta for 29 years, and is currently driving 757s and 767s. Quite naturally, the talk turned to sailplanes and general aviation. After all, nearly everyone who flies has had to start in something smaller than a Boeing, and that spells GA. And yes, he had fond memories of those hours in Pipers and Cessnas, and certainly his leisure hours in the sailplane still connected him to the business/sport of non-commercial, non-military aviation.

Even sailplaning has its share of government incursion, Neighbor pointed out, including the specter of requiring Mode C transponders and TCAS. It's not just the regulation that rankles everyone, but dollars and pounds are a by-product of electronic gear. Plus it requires power, and that would necessitate the added weight of a battery in a craft that's designed with a narrow payload and balance envelope.

Yeah, we agreed, who does the FAA think they are, requiring all that useless equipment in such a delicately integrated machine? However, in the next breath, Neighbor began extolling the inarguable virtues of GPS for pinpointing navigation, and more importantly proving the same to sailplane meet officials (via computer printout) where the aircraft has been on competitive flights. (Current proof is in photographs taken by cameras with fixed-focus lenses. The cameras, mounted on the wingtips, snap photos as points are passed.)

We wanted to ask Neighbor why he complained about avionics just a minute ago when there was the prospect of it being required, but now supports it when its features are beneficial. But we learned a long time ago that it is a waste of energy to argue with the IRS or PICs with 29 stripes on their sleeves. Despite his ties with general aviation, as the conversation progressed it was evident that Neighbor's sympathies were not wasted on it. He said business jets—particularly Citations, which are too slow and get in the way—should be banned from the airways that airliners use, etc.

Then, while swapping flying stories, we brought up one of our favorite subjects — crosswind landings. We, along with *General Aviation News & Flyer* columnist Alta Waddell, favor the cross-control, wing-low approach over the crabbed version, and as we loosely quote from one of Waddell's columns, "If you think the crab is the right way to do it, just think: Have you ever seen a 747 crab to a landing?"

Neighbor looked puzzled. "It's the way I do it in a 757," he said. "Been doing it that way every day for years. You lose too much lift in a cross-control. It's much safer to crab until the last second and then kick it around straight. Passengers like it better too."

"We prefer to set up wing low into the wind on final," we argued, "So we know exactly how much control we have to input to keep it straight. If you do it at the last minute, you're guessing."

As Neighbor suddenly turned and began fiddling with the winglet fitting, we realized that the conversation had become laden as if with rime ice. And then it dawned on us that here we were, giving advice to a man who made his living day after day doing what we do for free once in a awhile. Who's to say which of us was right? Maybe we both were.

While perusing the newspaper the next morning, we found an appropriate bit of advice in one of those "Thought for the Day" items:

"Socrates was a Greek philosopher who went around giving people good advice. They poisoned him." ✦

No Lawyers — These Two Settle at Arms' Length

DALLAS, Texas — In this litigious society, it is rare that even the most elemental of differences is settled outside the court system — even rarer when it is done with a sense of humor.

Southwest Airlines has recently been using the line "Just Plane Smart" in its advertising. It's such a good slogan that you wonder why no one has used it before. Well, it seems someone has. Stevens Aviation of Greenville, South Carolina had already been touting "Plane Smart" for several years, so some months ago Stevens' chairman, Kurt Herwald, gave a friendly call to the airline's boss, Herb Kelleher. Herwald pointed out the incursion.

Usually at this point various barristers are alerted, the clock is started, and everyone goes to work trying to blame someone else, preferably someone with a nice, deep pocket. Now we don't know Mr. Herwald, but we do know Mr. Kelleher, and while his solution to the problem was unique, it did not surprise us a great deal. Kelleher suggested a winner-take-all arm wrestling match, and Herwald agreed.

Kelleher is not your usual chairman of the board. The 61-year old has, in the past, dressed up as Elvis for an ad. Sometimes while flying on the Southwest 737s, he takes over for flight attendants, serving drinks and the airline's famous "meal" — peanuts. He often dresses in warm-up suits, although he never exercises — he smokes two packs a day, so what good would it do, he asks critics. Herwald, 37, does not smoke and exercises regularly.

Touted as the "Malice in Dallas," the epic match got gobs of free publicity from newspapers across the country, and from television networks such as CNN, ABC, the British Broadcasting Company, and others. After three months of good-natured taunting, the two squared off in mid-March at the Dallas Sportatorium, one of those tacky facilities usually seen on late night television as the site of grunt-and-bash wrestling bills.

Master of Ceremonies Randy Wristlock (a pseudonym used by Southwest's cargo manager), clad nattily in a tuxedo jacket, jeans, boots, and a yellow fright wig, introduced the gladiators to a live crowd of more than 1,000 spectators. Herwald was in street clothes, while Kelleher dressed in red "Everlast" boxing trunks over gray sweat pants, with his fighting arm resting in a sling.

Billed as a best-of-three-falls event, Kelleher substituted Texas Arm Wrestling Champion J.D. Jones for the first match, which he won handily. In the second, Herwald retaliated by choosing one of his female employees to face Kelleher. She took four seconds to pin Kelleher's arm and tie the event.

For the third fall, the real competition, the two men remained locked in combat for about ten seconds before the younger Herwald slammed Kelleher's hand to the table.

"I had a bad case of athlete's foot," Kelleher whined in defense of the loss. "I had a cold last week. I have a hairline fracture of my wrist. I think I overtrained when I ran up a flight of stairs the other day." After the post-bout posturing, Herwald gave back what he had just won.

"Just to show there's no hard feelings, or to be accused of taking advantage

Smokin' Herb Kelleher (left), CEO of Southwest Airlines, gives his all against Kurt Herwald, chairman of Stevens Aviation, during the "Malice in Dallas" arm wrestling bout over corporate slogans.

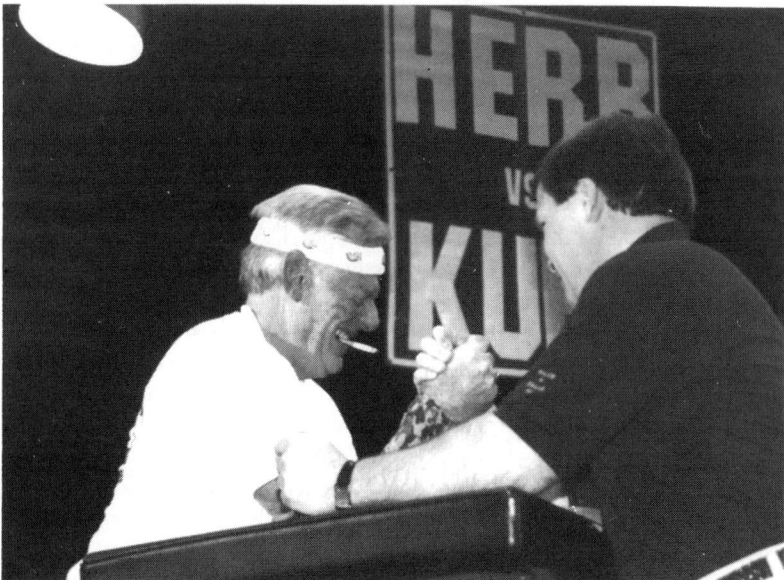

Photo by Tonda Montague

of senior citizens," he said, "we've decided to allow Southwest Airlines to continue to use our slogan."

The airline wasn't the only winner. The Muscular Dystrophy Association got a $10,000 donation from Stevens Aviation, and the Ronald McDonald House in Cleveland received $5,000 from Southwest.

And the public won, too. The legal system was spared the clutter of another time and cost intensive litigation, and the companies won't have to pass their legal fees and court costs along to customers. ✈

A 4,000-Mile Final From FL4000 With Zero Airspeed and No Power

CHESTERFIELD, Missouri — At the Aviation Safety Fair at Spirit of St. Louis Airport, several hundred pilots attended seminars on pre-flighting, go/no-go decisions, airspace reclassification, and avgas and lubricants. Attendees also reaped the benefits of a live fire-fighting display, Pinch-Hitter course, complimentary BFRs, and a "Never Again" panel. The fair was sponsored by the AOPA Air Safety Foundation, Phillips 66, and the Spirit Ambassadors.

After hearing the panel (comprised of pilots with an alphabet soup of ratings) and their true confessions, everyone felt that proper techniques and keen minds could handle just about any kind of scenario presented. However, when the afternoon's keynote speaker, Vice Admiral Richard Truly (retired astronaut, shuttle commander, and former NASA administrator), spoke of his NASA experiences and how they apply to safety in general aviation, everything suddenly paled by comparison. Truly described a 1983 mission he'd flown:

"At the beginning of the approach," Truly recounted, "the altitude was 400,000 feet, the airspeed indicator read zero, and the Mach indicator 25. The approach distance was something over 4,000 miles in a vehicle that had a landing weight of 205,000 lbs. and no engine — it was Space Shuttle *Challenger*, and there had already been several space shuttle landings, but this was the first one at night."

Likened to a flat rock, the shuttle has a glide ratio of 2.5:1 (two-and-a-half feet forward for every foot down), which produces an approach angle of nineteen degrees, flown initially at 290 kts.

While that may not sound too bad on paper, NASA found early on that the only real, live airplane which could successfully sustain that angle for training was the Gulfstream II, using both full power and reverse thrust! That angle and speed is flown to 1,750 feet above the ground and then "pre-flared" to a more normal one-and-a-half degree slope, flying at 185 knots to a touchdown 30 seconds later, "...just as you run out of altitude, speed and ideas," Truly joked. By the time of the night landing, Truly estimates he had flown 3,000 training approaches in the G-II.

The glide slope to the pre-flare point was held by reference to a VASI-type lighting system, with the final approach made with a ball/bar instrument and runway floodlights.

"The entire safety of the shuttle landing is designed in such a way that if you can consider that point in space where you go through pre-flare to be an 'energy knothole' — and you can pass the shuttle through that knothole at 19 degrees and 290 kts in the right configuration — you cannot land short. And you cannot have enough energy to land off the other end of the runway," explained Truly.

At 300 ft, Truly says he ordered gear down ("If you don't get three down and locked, you land with whatever you've got."), and he landed the shuttle, 50 feet long and two knots fast.

"The myth that astronauts and test pilots are brave is just that — a myth," Truly told the group. "They are taught that flying is a very risky business, and the way to survive it is to be educated, to train, to learn from other people's mistakes, and then to identify those risks and put everything possible in-between you and that risk, so when the day comes that you have to face it, you have as much protection as you can get."

Phillips 66 Aviation Marketing Manager Jack Hammond says his company is considering promoting additional safety fairs in conjunction with the AOPA Air Safety Foundation. As the country's largest supplier of fuels to general aviation, he feels that Phillips' involvement will ultimately help ensure a safer aviation system, which will benefit the general public.

The appearance of Dick Truly did a great deal toward reaching that goal. But even the commonest of us had one advantage over the Admiral.

"You know a lot more about general aviation than I do," he readily admitted. "Even though I've got about 6,000 hours, 300 carrier landings and two shuttle missions, I've never had a pilot's license!" ✈

Holy Hydraulic Oil, That Thing Wants to Eat My Airplane!

OKLAHOMA CITY, Oklahoma — If in the course of doing one's duty, one is requested to attend airshows, *this* one spends most of his time looking at the crowd as it cranes its tanned/sunburned necks at the featured attractions. Airshows are like rodeos: if you see more than two or three, you could pretty much say you've seen them all.

However, every time we are about to make sweeping generalizations about the aforesaid, up comes Aerospace America at Okie City, already voted best in the country and originator of the nighttime airshow.

Remembering back a few years to that first nighttimer, the big anticipation was who was going to do what, and how. I mean, an aerobatic act is great in the daytime, but who could even see it at night?

Steve Powell solved that with sparklers on the wingtips of his sailplane, creating a spectacular and graceful debut. Of course the warbird pyrotechnic crazies were there, rubbing their hands and anticipating the spectacle of recreating World War II *at night*, when they do their best work.

Anyway, this year's edition was eagerly anticipated at our house. We have somehow created a monster, taking Mrs. Ed — a term coined years aback when yrs trly was Supreme Editor of *General Aviation News* — to these shindigs. It used to be like prying molars to get her to the airport; now it is her momentum that propels us, and it was probably the nighttime airshow that changed her mind.

You haven't lived until you've spent eight hours on a 105-degree day at an airshow which has 30 acts and one porta-potty. But during the nighttime it's usually cool, and the winds are light, even in Oklahoma.

Opening with the Golden Knights, the show moved to standard aerobatic fare: Sean Tucker, Howard Pardue, French Connection, the Gee Bee, MDD's NOTAR helicopter, Bob Hoover and the Red Barons. At dusk, a pair of Ukrainian Su-29s lit up the twilight with their afterburners, and Les Shockley's three-jet Peterbilt dragster scorched the grass.

The nighttime performers have come a long way since that first show. Sean Tucker launched a fireworks display from his wing tips while flying a routine, Manfred Radius trailed Roman candles from his sailplane, Gene and Cheryl Littlefield did a floodlit wing-walk act, and the warbirds recreated the Battle of Britain with roughly the same amount of explosives as expended in the original.

Then came the *piece de resistance* — Robosaurus.

Forty feet tall and weighing 30 tons, it is a steel and hydraulic erector set dinosaur. With an 8,000-watt sound system, Robo rumbles and growls while it fires laser beams from its eyes and belches 20-foot flames and smoke as it menacingly opens and closes its jaws. I mean, it's as awesome as a rolling ball of butcher knives.

After rearing up and spinning around, and generally establishing its innate irritability, it suddenly found a hapless Aero Commander parked by the runway, ostensively a "drug plane." Robo moved toward it, lowered its head, and shot fire into the cabin. Then it picked it up and — I swear to Orville — ATE IT! Well, of course, it couldn't digest it, so there were pieces of aluminum falling all around, but it fair reduced that twin to a pile of trash.

Robosaurus has apparently been big on the fair and tractor pull circuit, and has been seen in a movie and on TV. But this, its first airshow appearance, and despite the fact that the display had little to do with flying, wowed the crowd. Of course, Aerospace America has been wowing crowds for many years, which is one of the reasons Mrs. Ed and us keep coming back.

We tried to do an interview with the robot dinosaur, but its handler said it had a date with a cute oil drilling rig it met earlier. ✈

Training For the Dog-Eat-Dog World of Corporate Aviation

Whilst at the NBAA Dallas shindig, we met the usual array of corporate pilot types. They were interesting and mostly employed and had good tales to tell, but none had the improbable background of Curtis W. Burt, chief pilot for Kimberly-Clark Corporation.

Curt told us he learned to fly in a club at Chanute AFB in 1968 while going to instrument repair school. When his tour was over, he went to Champagne Urbana and got a CFII, ME and Commercial. Then he moved to South Dakota, where he worked for South Dakota State University in the winter and sprayed crops in the summer. Then he relocated to Billings, Montana.

"I had my own airplane and did a lot of contract work for the Game & Fish Department," he explained. "It was a Super Cub, and I flew for game surveys:

antelope, elk, mountain goat, big horn sheep, and in the winter a duck and goose surveys on the Big Horn River, along with some transplanting. A lot of it was high-country work; the last job I did was a mountain goat survey. We spent about eight hours flying time in two days and never saw a goat below 10,000 feet."

Interesting work, but a stretch to see how it helped Curt in the cockpit of Kimberly-Clark's Canadair Challenger. But read on. In 1974 he moved back to South Dakota, to fly another Super Cub for the Game & Fish folk on a slightly different mission. "It was predator control," Curt concluded.

"I hunted coyotes. Basically, the majority of our work was keeping them away from the sheep ranches. There were 12 trappers and two airplanes and that's all we did year-around."

He explained that the state's damage control program, one of the largest in the country, was active only at ranchers' request, usually when they had a sheep kill. Curt worked in tandem with a state trapper on the ground while another one rode in the airplane as a gunner. We talked at great length about some of his experiences in the unusual role.

Like the cattle rancher who complained that the airplane was scaring his cows and forbade them to fly over his herd (coyotes usually prefer sheep) — until he found a calf which had been killed and partially consumed by a coyote. The rancher demanded they find the culprit. Curt and the trappers tracked down and shot the coyote, and upon performing a field autopsy, found the missing calf parts.

"The things we saw flying...some biologists who had been studying coyotes for 20 years hadn't ever seen," he said.

Curt flew the Super Cub about 2,000 hours in the four years he was a gunship pilot in South Dakota. Surely, we speculated, the coyote population was under control when he finished. "Naw," he said, laughing, "they had to get another airplane, and there's more coyotes now then when I left 14 years ago."

Curt moved to Appleton, Wisconsin to go to work in the right seat of Kimberly-Clark's King Air/Citation/Jetstar II fleet in 1978. He relocated in Dallas seven years ago when corporate headquarters were moved there.

Today, Curt keeps a coyote rug in his home as a reminder of his admiration for the animal. "I have a high regard for coyotes," he said. "They're a very sharp animal, and they'll be here long after we're gone. They're smart and adaptable."

✈   ✈   ✈

Loonies of Lancaster Build Outrageous Airplanes
November 1992

LANCASTER, Texas — Most of the year, the crew at Air Salvage of Dallas (ASOD) is involved in one aviation tragedy after another. Although founded as a salvage operation, Paul Camp and his crew quickly gained a reputation as the people to call for retrieval work after an accident.

Working with quiet efficiency, the ASODers move quickly to a crash site and, working with local and national authorities, carefully retrieve and remove every piece, store it and make it accessible for subsequent investigation.

It's sobering work being an airplane undertaker, so it's understandable that

Captain Ball Express *is one of the most unusual in a long line of "aircraft" from Air Salvage of Dallas. This extremely modified extended cab truck is fitted with folding wings, two jet nacelles, and much more.*

to keep their sanity, they have to be insane on occasion.

About 12 years ago, ASOD began an annual customer appreciation party — the customers being aircraft dealers and rebuilders, insurance companies, the EAA, National Transportation Safety Board members, lawyers, etc.

Someone came up with the idea of building an outrageous airplane to present at the gathering. Using bits and pieces, ASOD premiered its first product, the X-13. It was a Cessna 182 with an extra set of gear on top of the wings, a V-tail, and a "nuclear" power plant. Next came a guided missile, then an agplane built atop a Craftsman riding lawn mower, and finally a tilt-wing Jet Commander described by ASOD as a "machine with 150,000 moving parts surrounded by an oil slick."

Each model has somehow been built in total secrecy, and their star-spangled introductions have been worthy of any Cessna unveiling. The problem was, however, that it became harder to top the previous year, so ASOD decided to go another direction this year.

Camp loves to tell about the incident that inspired the 1992 model. Because ASOD uses trucks to transport aircraft on the highways, several years ago the U.S. Department of Transportation decided the operation needed some scrutinizing.

Logs had to be kept, standards met, inspections made. During one perusal of drivers' logbooks, a dismayed bureaucrat discovered that driver Richard Ball had made a 740-mile trip in 10 hours — with an airplane loaded on his fifth wheel trailer!

"That's an average of 74 mph!" the inspector said. "Didn't you even stop to go to the bathroom?"

"Sure," said the always-calm Ball. "Twice."

"This is not an airplane," the inspector growled. "If it was an airplane, we wouldn't even be here — that's out of our jurisdiction!"

The plot thickened. ASOD's Lucky Louque explained the process: "When I saw the DHL commercial on TV where they fly those delivery vans, I knew where we were goin'."

The lights went off at the Air Salvage party. The overhead doors opened, and in rolled Richard Ball's new mount, red lights blinking atop the cab.

"Here's the Captain Ball Express," yelled Lucky as the spotlights played on the bright red contraption, and the "Star Wars" theme swelled over the crowd's cheers.

The one-ton extended cab truck was fitted with folding wings (equipped, of course, with strobes, navigation and retractable landing lights) and two jet nacelles.

One of the first things needed at a crash sight is security, so the ASOD truck carried its own Rambo-esque paramilitary troops, complete with a roll of yellow "Crime Scene — Do Not Cross" tape. Because nothing can start until an official investigator arrives, a basic throw-down NTSB dummy was provided. And for the press, a rotating "eye in the sky" camera (complete with happy face) scanned the scene from above.

The assembled faithful gave the 1992 creation a standing ovation, acknowledging that the Loonies from Lancaster had put another one over on them — and maybe on the DOT, as well.

Now if they can just keep it from the FAA... ✈

What Some People Will Do to Get to the Super Bowl
February 1993

IRVING, Texas (home of the Dallas Cowboys) — Sending the 'Boys to a Super Bowl is nothing new in this town; they've done it five times previously — albeit the most recent may not have been in some of the earlier fans' lifetimes. But the mayhem that surrounded The Game in Pasadena seemed to generate more craziness here than the prospect of $40 oil. Within 12 hours of the NFC Championship victory, vendors materialized on every corner with logoed apparel proclaiming the feat, and you knew the T-shirt and gimmick cap producers were already putting the finishing touches on Super Bowl Champion artwork.

That most fans would do anything to watch their heroes in person is a given in any NFL town. But the value and scarcity of tickets does tend to separate the rich and/or famous from the rank and file, and the money from both.

So, to what lengths would people go to get to Pasadena? That question was answered when KVIL-FM, a local radio station which originates all Cowboys' games, announced that it was sending its "Traffic Patrol" Bell JetRanger to the game. The station would take along two lucky listeners on an all-expense-paid trip that included meals, lodging, hats, sweatshirts, $200 cash and a chopper ride from their hotel to the Rose Bowl, where the Super Bowl would be played.

The bright yellow JetRanger, which is leased to the station by All-Star

Helicopters, Inc. of Dallas, was scheduled to depart at 9 a.m. Thursday, so the promotion was termed a "suitcase party," one at which contestants showed up packed and ready to go.

Crowds began arriving at 6 a.m., and by 8:00 over 100 hopefuls were in place. A random drawing was held to cut the eligibles down to 20, and then a sports trivia quiz was held to determine the winner(s). The first question knocked out 18 contestants, and then the second question eliminated one of the remaining two.

That was good news to Jason Amyett, a 30-year-old Dallas accountant who had the right answer (he knew the alma mater of Cowboys safety Bill Bates is the University of Tennessee). The bad news was he and his friend Dana Kvapil would have to travel 1,500 miles in a cramped, four-seat kidney beater. At least the helicopter's range was mercifully short, which would offer a few moments' relief every couple of hours. Stops were scheduled in Abilene and Pecos, Texas, Tucson, and possibly Las Vegas.

The cozy confines of the "KVIL-icopter" posed another problem: Ms. Kvapil arrived with two large suitcases. Organizers quickly huddled and advised her to repack one to take along and they would send the other by airline.

As the Bell rejected the tarmac of the Texas Stadium parking lot and whop-whopped into the early morning air, two of the losing contestants busied themselves rearranging luggage in the trunk of their small car.

"We didn't win, but we're going anyway," said Tom Holman, who with his wife decided to just go ahead and drive to the Super Bowl. ✈

Chasing Comets in a Cessna 172

GRAND PRAIRIE, Texas — Bill Doran loves to fly, and he can come up with some very creative excuses to pull his Cessna 172B into the daylight and go poking holes. He says flying is great therapy, a good way to unwind from the pressures of the day. A Chicago native, he and his wife Jerry have lived in the Dallas area for a number of years, although not so long as to mistake them for natives. We met Jerry while we were appearing together in a musical; she introduced us to Bill at the cast party.

Last week during a regular meeting of the do-nothing club at a local eatery, we were lamenting the fact that another *General Aviation News & Flyer* column was due and we hadn't yet left town on a "Gadding" mission with the purpose of finding something to write about. In the midst of harassing a friend, an ex-Air Force pilot, for some flying stories, Bill walked in and sat down.

"Please say you've done something interesting in the last few weeks," we pleaded, knowing that Bill was never at a loss for a story or three.

"Well," he said, pausing to think, "Jerry did a gig as a back-up singer for Barry Manilow in a concert here, and then we went meteor chasing."

"Meteor chasing?"

'Yeah, the night of the great meteor shower. We flew out northeast of Dallas and looked for comets."

"Did you see any?"

"A few. They can scare you to death because they sometimes look like airplanes coming toward you."

Bill said he departed Grand Prairie well after dark, dutifully turned on his transponders and tuned in Dallas Approach Control to monitor traffic. Aside from the considerable traffic in the Northeast Quadrant trying to access D/FW International, Dallas Love Field, or one of a dozen other airports around the Metroplex, he recognized that perhaps seven or eight other small aircraft were making lazy circles around East Texas doing the same thing they were.

"We flew at 3,500 feet for a while, then climbed to 9,500," Bill said. "It was fantastic. The air was smooth, the temperature was way below what it was on the ground, and you could see forever. Seeing those comets from up there was like sitting in the tail gunner position on a B-29 and watching tracers."

Our other friend had been silent, but when a lull in the conversation developed, he leaned forward.

"There's just one thing that puzzles me," he said. "I don't think that Jerry even liked Barry Manilow."

"Maybe," Bill shot back quickly, "but it looks better on her resume than if she put down that she had sung with Murph." ✈

A Conversation With the Real J.R.

FORT WORTH, Texas—The citizens of this city like to promote its cowtown image, at least partly to better separate it in everyone's mind from its high-falutin' Eastern neighbor, Dallas.

Will Rogers may have hit the nail on the head. "If Fort Worth is where the West begins," the humorist observed during a visit in the 1930s, "then Dallas must be where the East poops out!"

It's notable that during WWII, Cowtown boasted the world's largest aircraft plant, the mile-long Consolidated B-24 factory, which later produced the B-26, B-58 and F-16. In the 1950s and 1960s the city was the site of the unofficial U.S. Aerobatic Championships, where Duane Cole and Charlie Hillard and a bunch of similarly inclined folk would gather once a year or so and fly until one was declared somewhat better than the others. Duane still holds forth a few miles south of town at Burleson, while Charlie spends his time between Eagles Aerobatic Team appearances and his auto dealerships.

And Fort Worth is also the home of J.R. Not the villainous J.R. Ewing, but Texas J.R.—three-time Indianapolis 500 champion Johnny Rutherford who, not surprisingly, is a pilot.

"I started out with an Aero Commander 200—the Meyers," J.R. said between bites of an Angelo's barbecue sandwich. "Then I had two P-51s. "

J.R. bought the first of the Mustangs in 1974, the year of his first victory at Indy. A few years later, he found a basket case P-51 at Chino, California, and had it restored there at Unlimited Aircraft.

"I used them cross-country," he explained. "I had always wanted an airplane I could do everything with." He kept the first airplane until about 1980 and sold the second one two years later and bought a Decathlon, which he later sold to Duane Cole.

"I had the good fortune to make acquaintance with my hero, Chuck Yeager," the 55-year-old retired racer related. "The first time I met him was when he drove the pace car at Indy. Somebody introduced us and the first words he said to me were, 'Yeah — you got a Mustang!'" They are still friends, and Yeager and J.R. go on yearly bird hunting trips.

J.R. comes by his passion for cars and airplanes honestly. His father worked for Funk Aircraft in Coffeyville, Kansas, and was chief mechanic for the Inman Bros. Flying Circus when young J.R. was born. The family moved to Tulsa after World War II, where the senior Rutherford became maintenance chief for the Oklahoma Air National Guard.

"That's when the racing bug bit me," he explained. "In Tulsa, my Dad owned a V8-60 midget race car — I grew up around race cars and airplanes."

In 1950, the Rutherfords moved to Fort Worth, and by the end of the decade, J.R. was driving modified stock cars at tracks around Dallas. In 1960, he accompanied Arlington, Texas racer Jim McElreath to the Midwest to race sprint cars and try to break into the big time.

"It was like it was predestined," J.R. remembered, "because that's what I wanted to do." He placed 8th and 5th in two IMCA feature races in LaCrosse, Wisconsin on his first try. "I made $180 and I thought to myself, how long has this been going on?"

Within two years, he was driving in USAC events, including stock cars, where he set a world closed-course speed record and won his first race. In 1963, he first competed at Indianapolis. His last attempt was 1992, when he missed qualifying by .003 mph in an uncompetitive car. In 24 starts at the Speedway, he had eight Top Ten finishes, including three wins.

The lunch crowd at Angelo's had come and gone while we visited. We walked to the parking lot, and there was little trouble spotting J.R.'s mount, a Chevy Suburban with an AOPA sticker on the rear window.

Parked next to it was an aging El Camino with a bumper sticker that elicited a chuckle from J.R. It read, "Foat Worth, Ah Luv Yew." ✈

7.

The World According to L.G. Poteet

Now it's important to realize that L.G. Poteet is a totally fictitious character created as an editorial diversion. His often outrageous stories and unique viewpoints of the aviation world served as a great source of humor, and whenever I wanted to nastily criticize someone or something via my column, I would just arrange for L.G. to telephone me and proffer his opinion. Rather than risk the alienation of an individual or company by stating my own opinions, I could rely on L.G. for his black and white, simplistic view of everything corporate, political, and/or moral. And even though it was patently obvious that he was not a real person, he often received fan mail — more, in fact, than the editor would.

When I was scheduled to talk to a non-aviation writer's group a few years ago, the chairperson asked me if my writing was considered fiction or non-fiction. After some thought about the persona of L.G., I answered, "semi-fiction."

How to Handle a Really Bad Drought

We've been in Texas just long enough to have noticed that we're beginning to lose that self-effacing quality which seems to have been inborn in Kansans. In Garrison Keilor's **Lake Woebegone Days** (Viking Penguin, 1985) a character named Harold Starr, who publishes the weekly *Herald-Star* in the fictional Minnesota town, thanks his parents with his *95 Theses 95,* a commentary on how he was raised:

"26. You taught me not to go overboard, lose my head, or make a big deal out of it, but to keep a happy medium, that the truth is in the middle. No extremes, don't exaggerate, hold your horses, keep a lid on it, save it for later. Be careful, weigh the alternatives, wear navy blue. Years later, I am constantly adjusting my feelings downward to achieve that fine balance of caution and melancholy."

Part of the problem overcoming that mindset while living amidst the, uh, outspoken and gregarious natives of the Lone Star State is helped by association with people like L.G. Poteet, a Texas Hill Country rancher, pilot, and part-time oil millionaire who feels that it's his duty to share his mind with us in the hope that we can at least rise to the rank of ex-Yankee.

The telephone rang, and as we picked it up we heard the unmistakable booming "HEL-lo" of L.G. (that stands for Laverne Gail, but only his mother is allowed to call him that). "I jist got my first copy of **Western Flyer & GAN**," he said proudly, "an' I see where you wuz up to Saynt Pawl foolin' with float planes!"

"Well," we said, "foolin' with isn't exactly what we did. We visited the Wipaire factory and saw a bunch of floatplanes, but we didn't get to fly any of them. How about you? Ever flown a plane on floats?"

"Shoot yeah, we had a buncha floatplanes down here on the ranch back in the Sixties," he replied, and I could hear his swivel chair squeak as he leaned back and put his Luchesses on the scarred top of the rolltop desk he claimed used to belong to Sam Houston. I plugged in the tape recorder (when L.G. is ready to tell a tale, it's about as obvious as rabbit pills in a sugar bowl).

"Wellsir," he began, "We wuz havin' our annual seven-year drought, an' all a the tanks (Texspeak for small ponds or watering holes for livestock) wuz dry as dust in a mummy's pocket. It was so bad that we had a three-year-old duck that'd never learned to swim!

"We converted some of our oil trucks fer haulin' water to the cows, but they kept gettin' stuck in the sand. So Wilmer — he wuz head of the ranch's flying department then — come up with the idea of buyin' some float planes. We could fly up to Lake LBJ, land an' fill 'em up with water, fly back an' land on the sand in the dry tanks an' unload the water!"

"What kind of airplanes did you get?" we asked. "Cessna 180s, 185s?"

"Naw, they wouldn't haul enough. We found a bunch of old DC- 3s, so we bought about a dozen of 'em an' flew 'em to Corpus an' had tanks installed an' put 'em on floats."

"Impressive," we interjected.

"Yeah, well, we did alright. We flew 'em to the lake, loaded 'bout a thousand gallons in each one an' flew in one humungous formation down t' the ranch. They all landed on the sand, an' we fair filled up one of them dry tanks."

"So it was a success?" we asked, knowing full well that the story was not over.

"Well, it was okay 'til we tried to take off in them puppies," he answered quietly. "We revved them Wrights to redline, but none of 'em Goony Birds moved so much as an inch in that sand! We tried pullin' 'em out with trucks an' tractors, but nothin' did any good, so we jist had to abandon the project an' go back to prayin' fer rain."

"So, those twelve DC-3s are still sitting out there on your ranch?"

"It's a funny thing. 'Bout three months later it started to rain. Poured down fer a week er more — musta been 20 inches. It began to flood, an' the water was real deep. I went over t' a neighbor's ranch to see if he was all right, an' there he was, standin' in water up to his armpits in what used to be his front yard. I sez, 'Can I help ya, Jake?' An' he sez, 'No, but you might give my horse a hand,'cause I'm standin' on his back!' Wellsir, when the rain finally started to clear off, we went out to see what happened to the DC-3s, an' all but one wuz gone — musta just floated away!"

"Did you ever find any trace of them?"

"Oh, I heard later that a family of bikers wuz livin' in one somewhere down by Matamoras, an' that someone had turned another one into a roadside diner near Brownsville, but I never saw it."

"What about the one that was left?"

"Well, you know, when it was rainin', it began to fill with all kinds of animals, an' the funny thing is that each kind wuz parin' off — a male an' a female — damndest thing I ever saw. 'Course, as soon as the rain stopped, they came out — two by two — an' we never saw 'em again!'"

"Wait a minute," we objected. "Is this a true story? There was a long, hurt silence on the telephone. Then with utter sincerity, L.G. replied, "Son, if I say a hen dips snuff, you'll find the can under her wing."

It's a true story. L.G. was there and he told it to me.   ✦

Nobody is Price Gouging
September 1990

We ran into our old friend, L.G. Poteet (South Texas rancher, aviator and part-time oil millionaire) over at Meacham Field in Fort Worth last week.

"Well," we said as he strode into Staci's Jet Center from where his Learjet was being fueled, "how're things goin' for you now that the price of oil is back up?"

"Wellsir, that's the good news," L.G. said as he took a roll of bills out of his Hart Schaffner & Marx cowboy-cut worsted wool pants. "It's been at $18 a barrel so long that we were gettin' used to it, an' now that it's pushin' $30, we seem to be about back where we started."

"I'll bet you hate to spend it all on Jet A, don't you? Do you think the oil companies are gouging us on fuel?" we asked, certain of a forthcoming opinion.

"Boy," he said as he pushed his Resistol back on his head, "you need a lesson in economics." He motioned me to a table in the customer area.

"Now Staci's here is chargin' about 24 cents a gallon more'n they were the first of August, right? They're doin' that because Exxon's probably charging them 24 cents a gallon more."

"So everybody's making money?"

"Lawdy, you can be so dense sometimes!" L.G. said disgustedly. "Okay, now...there's 42 gallons in a barrel of oil, so every time that barrel goes up a dollar, the raw material cost to Exxon goes up — let's see, divide one dollar by 42, boy."

"Two point three eight cents," I read on my handy dandy pocket calculator.

"Two point three eight cents," L.G. echoed. "Okay, so crude has gone up $10 a barrel so far this month, right? So ten times two point three-eight cents is..."

"Twenty-three point eight cents," I said without looking at the calculator.

"Right. So that's how much Exxon's raw material cost has gone up. Now, once again, how much higher is Staci's Exxon Jet A than it was last month?"

"Twenty-four cents. Oh, I understand, so no one is price gouging I guess."

"Well, unless you count me," he said sheepishly.

"What do you make of the Middle East situation?" we asked.

"Wellsir, Hussein wants the best of two worlds — to be left alone, an' at the same time, to control everybody else. He's kinda like a neighbor we had down in the Hill Country. He ran a herd of scrawny Hereford cows near one of our places, an' once in awhile one of his cows would get with one of ours. An' sometimes, if one of our prize Hereford bulls was around, well, you know what would happen. Anyways, after he was sure the cow had been bred, the neighbor would come foggin' down the road with the Sheriff in tow, accusin' us of rustling. But on the other hand, when one of our cows would get into his pasture, he'd say it was trespassin' an' he'd just keep it."

"So how did you get the guy to quit?"

"Well, one day at the sale in Austin we bought this awful lookin' Jersey bull an' took him over an' held up the fence while he went an' trespassed into the neighbor's pasture where he had a bunch of heifers. Before the guy found out about it, the damage was done. Come spring, he had a crop of the worst-lookin' Jersey-Hereford calves you ever seen! He couldn't hardly give 'em away! Durn near put him outta business.

"That neighbor an' Hussein are like my granddaddy used to say: 'A rustler who's never been chased by a posse thinks it's his right to steal.'"   ✦

One Man's Heaven May be Another's Hell

IRVING, Texas — The telephone blorted (phones don't ring any more), and we swung around from our morning regimen of trying to find inspiration in Dave Barry's column in **The Dallas Morning News** to answer it.

"That you? Are you there?" a voice shouted as we picked up the headset. No one but L.G. Poteet, South Texas rancher, pilot, and part time oil millionaire would ask such a question.

"L.G., how are you?" we asked as we reached for a pencil and pad, knowing something quotable would be forthcoming.

"Wul, I'm fine now that I know you're alive," he said with a sigh.

"What?" we asked, quickly thumbing through Section D, where perusal of the obits produced no one familiar. "Of course I'm alive! What makes you think I wouldn't be?"

"Musta been a dream," he said with uncommon quietness. "It was so real I jist had to check. You wuz there, big as could be, an' I talked to you an' everything."

No need to ask what he was about. He would tell anyway.

"I was flyin' that 600 horsepower Stearman I bought last year, see," he started. "I was comin' in over some scrub oak on the south end of a strip, an' I saw I was too low, so I pushed the loud pedal real hard, but nothin' happened. I thought I musta broke a cable or somethin'. No matter what I did, it jist kept sinkin' toward them trees, an' then — WHAM! — I hit one an' went cartwheelin' along.

"When I stopped, the airplane was all tore up an' on fire, but I wasn't hurt, so I jumped out an' started runnin', an' when I came around the trees, I saw a big airport with all these airplanes — old an' new, big an' small!

"I was walkin' toward a real slick P-51 that was bein' gassed up by a guy dressed in an Air Force colonel's uniform when I heard this rumblin' sound an' looked up an' there you wuz rippin' across the grass in one of them red Eye-talian sports cars! An' beside you in the seat was the most gorgeous woman I ever seen!"

"What kind of car was it?" we asked.

There was a silence on the telephone.

"It don't matter," L.G. said, disgusted. "You wanna hear the rest of the story?"

"Sorry. Go ahead."

"Anyways, you an' the filly got outta the car an' both started climbin' in the *Mustang*, so I go runnin' over to say who died an' made you rich, when you turn to me an' say, 'Did you work off the squawks on it, L.G.?' Well, I don't know what you're talkin' about, so you turn around an' holler at this young guy in a Delta Airlines captain's uniform up by the hangar, an' he comes runnin' down.

"You complain at him about the help he's gettin' nowadays an' tell him to go get the De Havilland out instead. He grabs me an' we go up an' drag this beautiful *Mosquito* out of the hangar an' pull the prop through a couple of turns, then you an' the gal git in it, start the Merlins an' take off. The Delta guy hands me a Crescent wrench an' tells me the annual on your G-IV is due before noon! I ask him if he can help, an' he says, no, he has to ferry your J-3 to Point Barrow!"

"Wow," we said, "that sounds like a real nightmare!"

"Nightmare nothing, it was Hell! Don'tcha see? I was bein' made to do the thing I hate most — not flyin'. As for the other guys, the Air Force officer was a line boy, an' the airline pilot was sentenced to fly a J-3 forever — wul, goin' to the top part of Alaska from Texas at 65 mph would **seem** like forever! "

"But what about the car and all those warbirds?" we asked.

"That was your heaven! You were gettin' to do the things I wanted to do, an' I was made to do the things I hated. Jeez, can you imagine goin' over a Gulfstream with a crescent wrench?"

"So what happened next?"

"I guess I woke up — musta been 'bout 15 minutes ago. Callin' you was the second thing I did!"

"What was first?"

"I rung up a preacher friend of mine an' said I'd be real interested in comin' to his church if he could give me directions on how to get there. When he asked why, I kinda told him about my dream, an' he said, 'Well, y'know, L.G., one person's heaven is another's Hell!'"

"Or put another way," we said, "one man's escargot is another one's slug. "

"Oh, Yeah! Now I remember," L.G. said proudly. "That's what the sports car was called — an Escargot." ✈

Why the Army Moved its Flight Operations to Texas

December 1990

"I don't know why everone's concerned about us fightin' a war in the heat an' the wind an' the dry in the Meddle East," complained L.G. Poteet over breakfast at Lucy's Lovin' Spoonful Cafe on the hard surface road near his ranch in the Texas Hill Country. "If they'd trained in Texas they'd be used to it. Hell, if you learn to fly out here, you can fly anywhere in the world!"

True, we reasoned, recalling L.G.'s windsock consisting of a four-foot long chain tied to a telephone pole. L.G. says that as long as the chain isn't horizontal, it's okay to fly. You have to believe that, too, because if you wait for the wind to die down to less than gale force, you won't fly very often in Texas.

"That's the reason the Army always trained pilots here," he added. "Breezes that'd break a windmill, ground as flat as a mashed cat, an' Pancho Villa."

"Hmm?"

"Pancho Villa. He wanted to be dictator of Mexico back before WWI, y' know, so he started a revolution. Wellsir, he decided to cross the border an' stir up a little trouble in the U.S. to get a little publicity, hopin' we'd retaliate against the gov'ment of Mexico. So on March 8, 1916 he raided Columbus, New Mexico, which is about 50 miles west of El Paso. An' the War Department sent ol' 'Black Jack' Pershing, 15,000 troops, an' six airplanes down to fight the ol' boy."

"What kind of airplanes?" we asked.

"Curtiss JN-2s," he answered, adding sarcastically, "it wuz a kinda underpowered version of the JN-4."

"Not too popular with pilots?"

"Nobody liked 'em, particularly the ground troops, 'cause the airplanes had a tendency to fall on 'em. On their first sortie into Mexico, one had to turn back with engine problems, one crashed, an' the other four had to land in the desert 'cause they couldn't get back to Columbus before dark. I mean, when you got a 40-mile headwind and an 80-mile per hour airplane, you gotta do some serious flight plannin'! By the end of the month, only two airplanes were left."

"So," we surmised, "aircraft didn't figure too much in the Pancho Villa campaign?"

"I wasn't finished," L.G. said with an impatient glare. "See, ol' Villa had airplanes, too, along with some American pilots he'd hired as, uh, consultants. A Wright biplane, a Curtiss pusher an' a Martin Type T. They used 'em just like we did, for reconnaissance, but their airplanes kept flyin' fer a whole year without one crash, not one forced landing!"

"Why do you suppose the Mexicans had so much better luck with their airplanes?" we asked.

"It weren't luck. Their pilots were from that part of the world, used to flyin' under the worst possible conditions—Tex-Mex weather. The U.S. Army's pilots, they were all officers an' gentlemen, y' know, from places like Tuxedo Park, East Hampton, Harvard n' Yale, an' places where they drank tea on Sunday afternoon out on the croquet court. They'd never seen conditions like they had in the Southwest. Their failure made the gov'ment decide that Texas, bein' about the worst thing they'd ever seen this side of Hades, might jus' be a good place to train all their pilots."

"You know all this for a fact?" we asked, suspicious of L.G.'s often-outrageous stories.

"Got it from my Daddy, who was there!"

"You don't mean he was one of the pilots?"

"Yep! "

"That's amazing. I didn't know he was ever in the Army."

"Wul, he wanted to be, but bein' a rawboned ol' Texas boy, they didn't consider him prime officer material. And 'sides, the pay wasn't too good anyway, so for $500 a month he sorta flew fer the other side!" ✈

Frontier Justice

HOUSTON, Texas — While waiting for a friend in the lobby of Owner's Jet at Hobby Field, we saw a familiar Learjet 25D squat to a stop on the ramp. And before its GEs had whistled to a stop, the clamshell doors opened and our old friend L.G. Poteet appeared on the airstair, resplendent in his ostrich Luccesse boots and straw Resistol.

"L.G.," we hollered as we waved and trotted toward the airplane, "what are you doing in Houston?"

"Wul, howdy, son," he bellowed as he grabbed our hand and pumped. "I might be askin' the same of you. I came down to pick up my new airplane."

"A new airplane? You getting rid of your Lear, or is it your Citation, Baron, 210, or what?"

"Naw, I ain't swappin' anything. I just bought a little runabout for ranch work — an Air Tractor."

"An Air Tractor?" we asked. "What in the world are you going to do with an agplane? You don't have anything but grass and rocks on your ranch."

"We got trespassers," he said. "You 'member the time we found a drug runner that was usin' one of our strips to make his drops?"

"Oh, yeah." We recalled the incident. After his foreman spotted the strange airplane, L.G. had jumped into a surplus Chance Vought F4U and proceeded to strafe the guy, which led to a meeting in Houston with several governmental agencies and the grounding of that particular airplane until it and its owner met with more civil standards.

"Well, when the bad guys found out my airplanes weren't armed any more, they started comin' back. So I figure I can use this here Air Tractor to stop 'em."

"You mean you're going to spray them?"

"Darned right! Oh, no parathion or malathion, or anything like that, just a kind of home remedy."

"Uh, what is it?"

"Oh, you know, some molasses thinned with a little Jalapeno juice."

"What'll that do?"

"Well, it should muck up the guy's airplane real good so he can't get away, an' if he gets any on him it'll probably draw flies an' cause blisters. "

"Frontier justice, huh?"

"Hey, if you fall in a cactus patch, you kin expect to pick stickers!" ✈

Visiting NBAA

HOUSTON, Texas — There are very few places at the NBAA Convention where one can hide from one's acquaintances and enjoy a few moments of peace.

The press room seemed safe and, in addition, there was a free buffet.

We were visiting with George Haddaway, retired publisher and industry gadabout, when we heard our name bellowed in recognition. We had been found by L.G. Poteet, erstwhile aviator, South Texas rancher and sometimes oil baron.

"Whaterya doin' here, boy?" he asked as he slapped us on the back, dislodging both a ham on rye with mayo and a partial plate.

"Well, L.G.," we said as we wiped the food off our lapels and adjusted the denture, "I work here. What's your excuse?"

"Jes' passin' through," he said as he moved someone's briefcase off the chair next to us and claimed the territory. "Thought I'd come over t' Houston an' see what wuz new in the world of aviation."

"L.G., I'd like you to meet someone," we said, suddenly inspired. "This is George Haddaway. He used to publish *Flight* magazine."

"Well, Mr. Haddaway, it's shore a pleasure," L.G. said, pumping George's outstretched hand. "My Daddy used to read *Flight* to me when I was just a pup."

"Say, L.G.," George said, putting his hand on Poteet's shoulder, "Do you know how to get the attention of a Texas oilman? You just snap your fingers and say, 'Oh, waiter!'"

L.G. laughed heartily and then launched into a counter-story. Our work here was done. They were having so much fun that we excused ourselves and headed for the convention floor.

An hour later, we returned to find L.G. drinking some of the free coffee and reading a press release.

"Well, did you and George get along pretty good?" we asked as we sat down.

"Salt of the earth, that man," he said. "Fer a publisher, he wuz a real nice guy."

"What do you mean, for a publisher?"

"Wul, son, I met a lot of airplane publishers an' editors over the years — the Collins boys, Lynton an' Mike..."

"I think you mean Leighton and Dick," we suggested.

"Whatever. Then there's Robin Leach from *Aviation International News.*"

"Wilson. Wilson Leach."

"An' of course there wuz ol' Tony Page who had *Cross Country News* outta Foat Wuth — now there was a magazine! An' Dave whatsisname from *General Aviation News & Flyer"*

"Sclair. "

"Yeah. An' who's that guy who publishes that paper out there on the Left Coast? *Pacific Flyer,* the one with all the half-nekkid girls hangin' on airplanes? Oh, yeah, I remember his name — Larry Flynt.

"No, you're thinking of the publisher of *Hustler,"* we suggested.

"All I know is there wuz a girl in there who reminded me of you — 'cept for the mustache, of course."

"I don't have a mustache."

"Exactly. "

There are very few places at NBAA where one can hide from one's acquaintances. ✈

8.

Last Flights

The "Gadding" columns I saved for last are probably the hardest I ever had to write because they are obituaries of people known and admired. In each case, when news of the death came, I immediately sat down and wrote the columns straight through, and sent them to be typeset without change. They were written from the heart rather than from the mind. They may be the best pieces I've ever written. I don't ever want to have to do another one.

There Once Was a Pilot — God, How He Loved to Fly!
July 1990

OKLAHOMA CITY, Oklahoma — *There once was a Pilot — God! How he loved to fly!* Ted Stranczek, Chairman of Oklahoma City's Aerospace America '90, was talking three days after we lost aerobatic pilot Tom Jones.

It was the first line of a verse Ted had penned the night after the airshow crash which took Tom's life, and he said it in the cavernous Hangar 9 at the FAA's Mike Monroney Aeronautical Center to the hundreds gathered for memorial services.

Years ago, we had met 1960-61 National Aerobatic Champion Harold Krier, and before we got to know him any better, he was gone. That day we selfishly vowed not to become friends with any aerobatic pilots because as careful as they were, one little miscue or distraction could have a fatal payoff and we would have to go through the grief all over again.

We'd forgotten that vow until Sunday. Tom affected you that way.

There once was a pilot. God, how he loved to fly! And made you want to fly, too.

We met back in 1983 when Tom was being sponsored by AAR Oklahoma and trying to establish himself in the airshow business. He was bright and brash and bubbly and intense, and instantly became your "best buddy," a term he always used instead of "friend" because it made you feel more special. Mrs. Ed was teaching reading in a junior high school and had an upcoming section on aviation, which utilized a liberal dose of "barnstormer" stories. She asked if we thought Tom would like to speak to her class about "stunt" flying, as the barnstormers had done. We asked, but Tom was so self-conscious about public speaking that he kept declining until we told him there was a free lunch and he could use a video tape of his routine for the presentation.

He was too shy to go by himself, so we met him at school, literally dragged him to the class, and introduced him. He hemmed and hawed for a few minutes, then loaded the homemade tape in the recorder.

"This is a show I did a couple of months ago," he said quietly. "Here I am doing what we call an aileron roll, and this is a loop."

The camera caught Tom's Pitts coming across the airfield. Suddenly the screen was filled with a blur and the sound track with unidentifiable noises and screams.

"That was supposed to be a snap roll," he said with a slight grin, "but the darned prop came off right in the middle of it!" The camera, obviously in the hands of a person who was on a dead run, caught the airplane as it disappeared into a dark hangar. A cloud of dust and debris emerged, and as the cameraman rushed inside, Tom was climbing out of what used to be a Pitts Special. He ran a few yards away from the wrecked airplane, then stopped and kicked his foot in its direction, disgusted.

We told that story to Kathy Jones, Tom's wife of two years, the day before Aerospace America opened.'

"That's not the Tom we know," she laughed. "Now we can't get him to stop talking!"

There once was a pilot. God, how he loved to fly. And talk about flying.

Although Tom was born in California, Oklahoma was his love. And when he started flying on the airshow circuit, narrating his own maneuvers from the cockpit, even the most hardened Easterners warmed to his Okie accent and phraseology. In 1986 he placed second at the Fond du Lac aerobatic competition, and the next year was signed to fly one of the Coors Light Silver Bullets. Tom captured the 1988 National Aerobatic Championship and was selected to be a member of the U.S. aerobatic team that won the World Championship.

He was appointed director of the first Aerospace America in 1986 and continued to run the show as well as perform in it for the next four seasons. The 1989 show was named best in the country. Earlier this year, he was inducted into the Oklahoma Aviation & Space Hall of Fame alongside astronauts and heroes like Wiley Post.

His final triumph was the securing of a major aircraft display and demonstration team from the Soviet Union. When the Sukhoi Su-26 was made available to Western pilots, Tom bought the first one to be sold in the U.S., and traveled to Russia last winter to tour the factory. Typically, he came home with a new set of "buddies," everyone from Russian mechanics to the chief of the Sukhoi Design Bureau.

When the Soviets came to Tom's airshow, they brought an awesome array of aircraft—two Su-27 fighters, an Su-26, a KI-32 helicopter and the world's largest airplane, the Antonov AN-225. The Friday evening, Saturday and Sunday shows drew 200,000 people to Will Rogers World Airport.

There once was a pilot. God, how he loved to fly. And share flying with the world.

Boris Rakitin, Chief Sukhoi Designer and leader of the Soviet delegation to Oklahoma City, read a cable from the head of the Russian aircraft bureau. The wire said the entire Soviet Union had been watching with delight as their fliers and our fliers became friends through this trip, and the Russian people were tremendously saddened over the loss of their good friend Tom Jones — or as they called him, their "little friend," a reference to Tom's height.

In the moments after the Sunday crash, that grief was personified by Russia's star military pilot, Pogatchev, who sat on the main gear wheel of his Su-27, weeping openly.

As Tom's "Rush 'n Rage" lay crumpled and broken in a blackened circle of grass in front of the disheartened crowd, the Soviets quietly mounted their aircraft and made a solemn fly-by. No fancy aerobatics, no words, just lots of emotion.

Moments later the U.S. Air Force and Air Guard saluted with a procession of 25 aircraft: helicopters, F-16s, A-7s, A-10s, C-130s and a lone B-52. Without suggestion, the crowd quietly filed to their cars and went home to reflect on what it all meant. ✈

The Gulf War Strikes Next Door
February 1991

IRVING, Texas — After the start of the Gulf War, Americans discovered that not everyone at home was prepared.

We forgot that our young children have never had to react to a genuine war. You have to remember that up to junior-high age, most kids do not have a well-developed sense of the world, distance, geography, and/or political boundaries (nor, according to most experts, do some high schoolers).

To them, Saudi Arabia could well be in the next county, and Saddam Hussein might make his headquarters in that deserted barn out by Uncle Harry's farm. Despite the fact that kids have always played at killing and/or have been generously exposed to death by the media, they are often able to tell the difference, and the real thing can scare the bejeebers out of them.

It's not just children who may be unprepared. Reality came closer to our home early one morning in late January. We were awakened at 3:30 a.m. by footsteps and voices. Fearing that prowlers were about, we got out of bed to investigate. As we peered through the drapes from our upstairs bedroom, we saw three shadowy figures standing on our next door neighbor's porch. We were about ready to call 911 when the porch light came on and we saw that the trio were Marines. There could only be one reason why they were there in the middle of the night.

"Oh, God," Mrs. Ed whispered. "Why couldn't it have just been burglars?"

Lance Corporal Daniel Walker, the men solemnly informed his mother, was one of the 11 Marine casualties at Khafji.

By the time the sun had started its daily cycle, the street was becoming crowded with cars and vans, each sprouting multiple antennas, satellite dishes and news department logos. The reporters who came and went throughout the day were the same people we always ran into at press conferences and disaster sites, but that day they seemed different.

A burly cameraman quietly laid his equipment down upon entering the house and embraced Daniel's mother in a silent, tearful hug. The scene was repeated again and again throughout the day as the normally calloused, hardened reporters and technicians let down their professional barriers and became emotionally involved with a person who, until a few hours earlier, had been a total stranger.

These people were in the same business as the correspondents we'd watched for weeks on television — those who kept asking unanswerable questions and making assumptions and demanding that the people had a right to know.

Those people seemed to just be concerned with statistics. How many hundreds of thousands of personnel, how many tons of bombs, how many *Patriot* missiles? But the people in the living room next door were immersed in the reality of a single life.

Dan's mother was vainly trying to cope with the death of her only child, the one who now had the dubious distinction of being the first soldier to die in combat in the Persian Gulf War.

"It parallels his life," she said. "When he was a kid, whenever he did something wrong, he always got caught the first time. That's how he was. You know how some kids can do things forever without getting caught? He always got caught."

When she had talked with him on the telephone a few days earlier, he had promised her that he would be home soon, and when he did come home, he would dress up in his Marine blues and take her to a restaurant where he would order a beer.

But, she had told him, he would have to wait another year for the beer — he wouldn't be 21 until New Year's Day 1992. ✦

One Last Adventure

WICHITA, Kansas—It was a flight that you hopefully only have to make once in your lifetime, and you can't find anyone who can tell you how to handle it. At least there was no one at Midwest Corporate Aviation on Jabara Airport who had ever done it when we rented the C-172, clutching a small plastic box containing the ashes of our best friend.

Tom Chandler, a young instructor working on a Wichita State University Aviation Management degree, rode right seat, as we didn't have time for the compulsory check ride. Our best friend's widow and daughter were in the aft seats.

It was good to get back into the old Skyhawk. How many years had it been since we'd flown this, our learning plane? If it would have only been a more somber color. Its lavender stripe distinguished it as hopefully the only one of its kind in existence. As we rolled down the runway, we pulled back on that skinny little control wheel horn and lifted smoothly into the ever-present crosswind and leveled off about 1,000 feet above the ground, headed for the Emporia VOR and the Flint Hills. It was a route Terry had flown countless times when he was in the oil business and owned a Beech Sundowner.

An hour earlier, at the memorial service, we had told of our great adventures together. It was just like **Lonesome Dove**, we had said, and we were Gus and Woodrow, the two of us. He plotted and planned his successes, worked hard and prospered. On the other hand, yrs trly acted more impulsively and tried a wider variety of things, although we never seemed to achieve any particular goals. Either because of or despite our differences, we'd had some great adventures.

We could sit for hours together without speaking, a habit which drove our wives crazy. We once attended a national motorcycle rally in Colorado together. Terry grew impatient with the crowds and quietly announced that he was going off for a couple of days to ride through the mountains. We stayed, although his departure made sense to us. When he returned early the next morning, we asked why he had come back so soon.

"I got tired of not having nobody *not* to talk to," he grumbled.

Terry collected philosophies—everything from those little fillers in **Reader's Digest** to elaborately framed pieces. They covered the walls of his office.

The night after his death, we sat at his desk reminiscing. Under a corner of the desk pad were some scraps of paper. We picked one up, and it was as if it was there for us to find: *Mourn me not, I chose the path.*

"There's Emporia," Tom said as he pointed over the nose of the Skyhawk to the clutter of homes which interrupted the rolling, treeless hills of East Central Kansas.

The written instructions which Terry had left us specified the spot, and we had marked it on a sectional. It was a bare and beautifully grassy hill. All that remained was seeing if our aerodynamic presumptions would get the job done successfully.

"Give me about a thirty-degree left bank at 500 feet and slow it to 60 or so without too much flaps," we yelled to Tom.

We opened the box, and inside was a small plastic bag filled with ashes. We had planned on simply unlatching the door and scattering the contents from the opening at the rear, but the seat was too far forward to accomplish anything gracefully.

"I'm going to have to open the window," we said to no one in particular. At least it was something we could reach, and we began letting the air flow pull the ashes out. After two complete turns, we closed the window and headed back to Wichita. We had accomplished the most difficult thing surrounding a death. We had let go of a life.

One of the clippings Terry left may have explained it better:
Him that I love, I wish to be free — even from me. ✈